S0-AQM-515

ROSIE'S PLACE

ROSIE'S PLACE

Offering Women Shelter and Hope

ANDREA CLEGHORN

VanderWyk & Burnham
Acton, Massachusetts

The names of Rosie's Place guests, interns, and noncorporate staff members have been changed to protect the privacy of individuals described in this book. All events, however, are truly reported.

Published by VanderWyk & Burnham
A Division of Publicom, Inc.
Acton, Massachusetts

Library of Congress Cataloging-in-Publication Data
Cleghorn, Andrea.
Rosie's Place: offering women shelter and hope/Andrea Cleghorn.
p. cm.
ISBN 0-9641089-9-2 (hardcover)
1. Rosie's Place (Boston, Mass.) 2. Women's shelters—Massachusetts—Boston—Case studies. I. Title.
HV1447.M4C54 1997
362.82'9283—dc21 97-28109
CIP

Acknowledgment is gratefully given for permission to include these works of others: **Songs:** "Somewhere" from musical *West Side Story*—words by Stephen Sondheim, music by Leonard Bernstein; Chappell & Co., Inc./G. Shirmer, 1957. "Camelot" from musical *Camelot*—words by Alan Jay Lerner, music by Frederick Loewe; Chappell & Co., Inc., 1960. "Money (That's What I Want)"—words and music by Berry Gordy, Jr., and Janie Bradford; copyright 1959 Jobete Music Co., Inc.; "Rock 'n' Roll Music"—words and music by Chuck Berry; Arc Music Company, 1957. **Photographs:** Andrea Cleghorn—pages 80-D (bottom), 80-E (middle left and right), 80-F (bottom), 80-G (middle, bottom right); Robert Gillis—page 80-H (bottom); Janet Knott—pages 80-A (all), 80-E (top, bottom), 80-F (top), 80-G (bottom left); Narrow Gate—page 80-D (top, middle); Amy O'Doherty—page 80-H (top); Arthur Pollock for the *Boston Herald*—pages 80-B (top right), 80-C (all); Rosie's Place file—pages 80-B (bottom), 80-G (top), 80-H (middle); Jonathan Sachs—page 80-F (middle); George F. Weinstein—page 80-B (upper left).

Book design by Ruth Lacey Design

Manufactured in the United States of America
10 9 8 7 6 5 4 3 2 1

For Abby and Alex

ACKNOWLEDGMENTS

I AM GRATEFUL FOR THE HELP of everyone at Rosie's Place, for the willingness of guests, staff, and volunteers to share their stories with me. I thank Kip Tiernan and Julie Brandlen, who encouraged me along the way, never wavering from their dedication to respecting women's dignity.

My appreciation goes to Pam Besold for on-the-job training; Tom Wilson for all the letters; Eileen Doyle, who provided a quiet place to work away from the heat; Becky Frank and Dick Montgomery for reference assistance; Mickey Hinkle, who always recognizes a good story; Meredith Rutter for taking a chance; and Barbara Shapiro and Carole Vogel for helping out at the very beginning. I am indebted to Marjorie Waters and Onnolee Sullivan, who were never very far away, to Janet Knott for coming to shoot the great photos, and to Ira Shull, my wonderful editor.

Thanks go to my son, Alex, a first reader whose view on the world helps me notice things I never otherwise would, and to my daughter, Abby, a true companion, who is present in so much of my work.

CONTENTS

PREFACE

I FIRST CAME TO ROSIE'S PLACE in January of 1994 on assignment for the *Boston Herald* to write a Sunday magazine piece. It was for the anniversary of the founding of Rosie's Place, Easter Sunday twenty years before. I knew that Rosie's Place was the first emergency shelter for women in the country, but like many people in the Boston area, I had only a hazy idea of the work being done or even of the population being served. Was Rosie's Place for homeless women? Yes, but not only. Was it for battered women? Too many times, yes, but thankfully not always. What I found was that Rosie's Place is dedicated to women who need help. The mission statement says it simply: *to provide a safe and nurturing environment for poor and homeless women to maintain their dignity, seek opportunity, and find security in their lives.*

Not far into the research for my *Herald* story, I knew I wanted to write more about Rosie's Place. Founder Kip Tiernan quotes Melnea Cass when she says, "If we cannot do great things, let us do small things in a great way." Sociologists, economists, and psychologists have written comprehensive and insightful books on homelessness; I have written this book to show how a small place is accomplishing great things by helping women one at a time. It is

Rosie's Place seen through the perspective of a few of the women involved—volunteers, staff members, and benefactors as well as guests.

Soon after my story in the *Herald* was published, permission was given to come inside by Kip Tiernan, Executive Director Julie Brandlen, and the board of directors. I started spending time at Rosie's Place. I stayed overnight; I hung around during the day. I went to board meetings, staff meetings, and all-day planning meetings. I went to talent and fashion shows starring Rosie's Place guests. I attended the Share Your Heart party in February and Kip's seventieth birthday party in June of 1996. I met with volunteers in the suburbs—in Concord and on the North Shore. I helped a woman with essays for her English class, and I read to children so their moms could eat lunch. I worked on the newsletter, collected trial-size soaps and shampoos for the hygiene drawer, and ran an orientation meeting for volunteers. I took time from my own family to celebrate some of Mother's Day, Thanksgiving Day, and Christmas Day at Rosie's Place.

In the end, much of my research took place in the dining room at Rosie's, where I worked the Friday lunch shift for two years, and in coffee shops where I met women to talk. The symbol of Rosie's Place is a coffee cup with a rose. The coffee I knew about. The flower came later.

One sunny June morning, I picked up a Rosie's guest at her apartment and we headed out to have lunch. We had spent enough time together that at this point, my needing to do more research for her story was just an excuse to get together with someone whose company I enjoyed. Along the way, she asked me to stop the car at an apartment building where she knew the custodian. He had been putting in flowers and had let her know he had some extras. He said she could give the plants to her landlady, who might give her a few days' grace on the rent.

She put a couple of pots in the back of my car, then handed one to me. I initially refused, thinking she should use all the plants she had for goodwill at home. She insisted, saying, "I never have anything to give to you. Please take it."

Over the months we had known each other, I had seen her thrown into situations that would defeat most people. I was in awe of how she managed, as her courage and resiliency were tested over and over again, but she kept going—and with an amazing sense of humor. She never had much money, and funds were particularly tight that morning when she wanted to give something to me. It was important for her to be able, for once, to do that. The plant grew and eventually blossomed on my front porch, a gentle reminder of the desire to nurture as well as to be nurtured.

ROSIE'S PLACE

PROLOGUE

Kip Tiernan at Community Church

"We in the city see the forces of evil colliding in the most raw forms. We see the faces of the poor, empty, sad, disaffected, disillusioned, and, Christ knows, the crazy. It is here at the core that the strength or weakness of the city is most accurately measured."

BOSTON, MASSACHUSETTS—JANUARY 1994. The voice of Kip Tiernan, the founder of Rosie's Place, is raspy from decades of smoking unfiltered cigarettes. With her bright orange sweater, Hush Puppies, and Greek fisherman's style black cap, Kip is a small but mighty presence in the stark meeting room that is the Community Church of Boston. On this bitterly cold, sunny Sunday morning, men and women of the church have climbed two steep flights of stairs to hear Kip, who is the guest speaker. Their new minister has advised them to keep their coats on. It is the coldest day of the new year, and last night the furnace stopped functioning.

"Shelters and soup kitchens," Kip continues, "are the burnt offerings of the twentieth century." She is referring to the prophet Amos, who rejected as hypocrisy the sacrifices brought to him. "Amos said, 'Let justice run like a river.' Well, Amos would find it tough sledding on Boston Common right now." Speaking of President George Bush's campaign for individuals and communities to get directly involved, Kip goes on, "Amos would not accept the burnt offerings. There were not a thousand points of light for Amos."

Kip opened Rosie's Place in the early 1970s, twenty years earlier, when she realized starving women had nowhere to get help. Working in an urban ministry at St. Philip's in Boston's South End, she had seen women masquerading as men to get a meal at the all-male Pine Street Inn. When she had called city hall for information about what was being done, she was told there were no homeless women in Boston. But Kip knew better.

She found an abandoned storefront, once known as Rosen's Family Market, on Columbus Avenue and leased it. She had no special affinity for the Rosens, but, to her, the name sounded friendly—it made her think of a favorite aunt's kitchen or a coffeehouse. She wanted to avoid a name that in any way sounded institutional. For a couple of weeks before the opening, Kip handed out small pink flyers that read, "Need a meal? Come to Rosie's Place." She gave them out by the handful and asked women on the street to spread the word.

Kip put the coffee pot out for the first time April 14, 1974. She picked Easter Sunday because "it sounded good, sort of a resurrection." There wasn't too much to offer women that first day, just coffee, sandwiches, and soup. Still, with the help of a check for $250 from two suburban women, Rosie's Place, the first emergency drop-in center for women in the country, had begun.

Now, two decades later, Kip tells the congregation that she has seen homelessness become a market with its own pedagogy. "The subject of homelessness is taught by people who wouldn't touch a homeless person with a barge pole." She adjusts her cap for the third time and says that Harvard University is offering a course in shelter management. "*Cui bono?*" she asks. "You've got to ask who benefits." Would the people at Harvard waste their time if they didn't think this was a market?

"We've moved from caring and compassion in the 1970s to compassion fatigue in the '80s to dismissal in the '90s. To blame those already on their knees says something about us and them." Nods of agreement go through the room. Kip stops for a moment and chews thoughtfully on her gum.

Continuing, she tells the group that a decent standard of living is what has to happen for women in Boston. Poverty, she says, is not an emergency, it is an economic condition imposed on a particular class. She picks up speed, her blue eyes flashing. "We have adopted an extraordinary hostility. 'Get those bums off the street!' Where do the homeless go now? What do we do with them? We've written checks, we've donated our clothes, we haven't changed anything. Bad politics create bad policy. We need you to blow the whistle on the politicians. They are interested in spins and photo ops."

There were two shelters in Massachusetts in 1982, Kip explains to the congregation. Now, in 1994, there are 170. The number of shelters has grown proportionately with homelessness, which is increasing in Boston at a rate of 25 percent per year. "We can't fix this with more shelters! Homelessness is increasing in Boston and the biggest group is the kids—what do we do, kill them?"

She leans up against the lectern, beseechingly, confidingly. A few motley space heaters, each with a distinct rhythm and voice, spew out warm air. "I miss the collegial caring we once had. We didn't always win, but we knew we were alive, we were taking a stand. We had heroes and heroines then, whistle-blowers. Back then we had Emma Goldman and Mother Jones and Rachel Carson. Today, fax machines have replaced fury, retreat has replaced rage, conference has replaced confrontation. We indulged in childish dreams then, such as stopping wars. We started peace movements, civil rights movements. We had visions; now we have agendas.

"At Rosie's Place we love everyone unconditionally—God knows we may not like some of them! [Kip chortles.] When we infantilize people because it makes our job easier, we lose our humanity. I hear someone say, 'Is she house-ready?' and it makes me think of house-broken. I get mad when I hear the word 'intake'—what happened to hello?" Her small hands grip the lectern.

Kip, getting by on $11,000 a year, calls living on the edge her "preferred geography." An enormous silver cross hangs on a chain around her neck; it's her trademark, a visual reminder of her connection with St. Philip's parish.

"In this new year, be healers of the sick, the broken, the suffering; put this pitiful world in caring hands. Don't bother to fix it—change it, so that no child's dream is deferred, so that no poor woman is alone and lonely.

"I have this rage, I have this hope. I want to reclaim the vision, not for eternal life but for life now. I'm not a visionary, just a tired old lady trying to do the best I can. We need to transform society now. We need to move from being do-gooders to good-doers to eliminate the causes of suffering."

1

BEACH

Julie Mason, a Rosie's Place staffer, waits by the door of a chartered air-conditioned bus. Clipboard in hand, she is checking women's names on her list as they climb aboard. Julia Lee, an intern, here for the summer from Yale, is with her.

It is a few minutes before nine on a sunny July Wednesday morning in Boston's South End. A cloudless blue sky promises stifling heat by afternoon. At this hour, the bus parked in front of Rosie's Place is the center of the only real pedestrian activity on the street, which includes expanses of empty parking lots and a fortress-like shoe factory. Down the block, Blanchard's liquor store hasn't opened yet, but a handful of people are hanging around outside, leaning on shopping carts and waiting. A few scraggly weeds growing out of the cracks in the sidewalk are the only greenery in sight.

Julie and Julia are as different as their names are similar. Staffer Julie is tall, solid, and sad-eyed, with a long Irish face. Intern Julia is tiny and energetic, with shiny black hair that swings perfectly into place with every move of her head. No one has managed to keep their names straight, and by this stage in the summer the two women have stopped bothering to correct people. Their jobs are similar—to act as advocates for the guests.

The women climbing into the bus range in age from their twenties to their seventies; some are carrying bags, others are traveling considerably lighter. All seem glad to sink into the seats, where it is at least fifteen degrees cooler than outside. Standing at the top of the steps, the driver, a tall congenial-looking guy with faded, reddish colored hair, greets the women and helps them climb up. As if by some kind of agreement, the front of the bus becomes populated with women who keep to themselves. Scattered and silent, they sit one to a seat that would hold two. In the back, the women crowd in together, talking.

"You know who the driver looks like? Bill Weld!" says a back-row sitter.

"You are right about that!" They laugh at the idea of the governor of Massachusetts taking them to the beach for the day.

The driver introduces himself as Adam. When everyone is seated, he jokes, "Now I just want to make sure everybody's on the right bus. This one is going to Atlantic City, so I hope you have lots of money!"

This brings more laughter. "Hey, I don't have any money!"

A few minutes later, the bus is rolling toward the expressway. Out the window the passengers can see the neighborhood change to an area some of them have just come from, full of weathered triple-decker houses with sagging porches, brick apartment buildings with cement courtyards, and warehouses interspersed with overgrown vacant lots. After a mile or two, the bus climbs onto the highway. A suburban church group has invited the women of Rosie's Place to visit for the day. The plan is to stop at the church rummage sale, spend some time at the beach, and then return to the church for a barbecue.

One woman is trying to start a conversation with her seatmate, but it isn't working.

"Looks like a good beach day."

There is no response, so she tries again.

"Have you gone on any of these trips before?"

"Look," the other woman says, without making eye contact. "It's free. That's why I'm here. If there is coffee and doughnuts, that's just great. But mainly I'm going because it's free." She turns to the window and doesn't turn back.

Adam turns out to be a better entertainer than navigator. It takes a while before the correct exit is found, and after that there are a few more missed turns. At one point, he announces, "We may be lost, but we're making great time!" Some of the women mutter at this, disgusted, but the crowd in the back has gotten so loud that most of them miss his comments entirely.

Women are ducking in and out of the bathroom at the rear of the bus to put on bathing suits, each change the object of scrutiny. "Where did you get that thing?" Upstairs in the clothing room at Rosie's is the reply. "Whew, well I guess my problem is I'm not, you know, real big on all those rhinestones."

Finally Adam gets the bus on the right track, entering the heart of the leafy South Shore community they are visiting today. He turns down a street lined with white Colonial houses and drives past the common with its traditional meeting house. "We're getting so close I can smell the coffee from here," Adam says, as the bus approaches the church. He pulls into a space by the front door. In the parking lot that runs alongside the church, tables and folding chairs are set up in the shade. Pink-and-orange doughnut boxes are piled on the tables next to urns of coffee.

The women of the church bustle around. Some of them talk to, but most do not sit with, the women from Rosie's, who have settled into chairs. Conversations are in shorthand; there is not much in the way of formal introductions. Talkers are in bigger supply than listeners. Soon some of the Rosie's women are bored; others put up invisible "do not disturb" notices. Those who feel chatty sit together, talking and laughing, until everyone is offered the chance to preview the rummage sale that has been set up inside. They are invited to take whatever they want, with one practical exception: "Please, no bikes!"

Inside, the tables are loaded with clothing, kitchen gadgets, shoes, board games, and miscellaneous household items. One woman tries on a pair of hot pink warm-up pants over her bathing suit. "Oh, girlfriend!" is the group response. Taking this as a positive, the woman stuffs the pants into one of her bags and then walks on to look through the small appliances. She starts testing an alarm clock.

Other women play show and tell. Someone displays the red drapes she has selected; another holds out a miniature scales of justice; a third shows off a typewriter and some glassware. One woman holds up a big Plexiglas double-picture frame: "I saw this in Filene's for fifty-eight dollars!" she exclaims.

A tall, slim woman with huge dark eyes and a small ponytail talks about how her one-year-old son runs through the house ripping everything up. "I miss him today," she says. "I'm used to having him with me all the time." She looks at some toddler-size overalls, then goes through a pile of shirts for her older children.

Outside, having previewed the sale, the back-of-the-bus group congregates at one of the tables, eating doughnuts. Sarah Rose, a Rosie's volunteer, knows several women from the church because they bring a meal to Rosie's Place once a month. She sits down with them and begins to talk to a newcomer at the table. "Look, I've been clean for a year and four months," she says, extending both forearms to show. "It's been the hardest thing I've ever done."

~

SARAH ROSE WENT INTO RECOVERY January 12, 1993, a date never far from her mind. She remembers when she hit rock bottom. Her two young sons were being taken away from her. "They were all I really had." She had few options: go to work, go to school, go to jail, go into a drug program. She took the program.

Sarah is from Brockton, a small industrial city south of Boston. Growing up, she spent time in foster homes. At one point she was put up for adoption, but she ran away. "Everyone in my family was doing drugs when I was growing up," she says. "I'm not using this as an excuse, but it's important. I guess you would call mine a dysfunctional family."

She has a mother, a brother, and three sisters. She says her mother gave her what she could at the time, but she just didn't have much to give. No one did. "My mother was very poor," Sarah explains. "I don't think she even had love to give me. Everything she did in the past is over. My mother did the best she could, I give her credit; today she's my best friend. But I still suffer."

Sarah has tried residential drug programs, halfway houses, and a drug treatment facility in the past. At the facility, she got into some trouble because she was angry—she picked fights with people. She says that she's a very angry woman. "I'm a child in an adult body. It comes out. I let the child out. It never got out when I was a kid. Even though I understand the past,

I still need—well, I do the best I can and try to help people a lot."

One day Sarah came to Rosie's for a meal with a friend and met one of the staffers. She liked the woman and began volunteering at Rosie's, first in the dining room and then in the clothing room. At the time, Sarah was living with a man she was abusing and who was abusing her. She was always in tears. Finally, one day someone came up to her and said there was a bed available if she wanted to stay at Rosie's for a while. "I couldn't believe someone would come up to me and just offer me a bed. I hadn't even asked. That was a Friday. I moved in that night."

The overnight program at Rosie's Place is set up for women to stay a week, but they may stay longer if they are working on a goal. The goal may be to find a place to live, or it may be to get into recovery. Sarah stayed for seven weeks. "I really didn't feel I was working on a goal at all." For Sarah, Rosie's Place provided a reprieve, a place to rest.

Sarah says in general she doesn't really like women and insists she prefers to be alone. Still, the two months at Rosie's were a good time for her. "I loved it there. They gave me money, treated me good, gave me food. We had a good crowd up there. I had fun! If I could go back to it, I would."

Despite the good times, Sarah says Rosie's plan was not set up to make it comfortable for her to stay. She knew she needed to find something more permanent. When it was time to leave Rosie's, she filled out twenty housing applications in four hours. She moved into a room in one of the lodging houses connected to another shelter a mile away. Unlike her room at Rosie's, this room came with a key and a bill that had to be paid.

It wasn't as good as Rosie's; she didn't like the people as much, she says. Still, she stayed there for fifteen months, then finally got her own apartment.

Every gain in Sarah's independence has been matched by a responsibility to be met. "That was so hard, being on my own in an apartment. Instead of one bill, I had four. I had to pay rent, lights, gas, and phone. All of a sudden I had to do everything—take out the trash! It was really hard for me."

Now Sarah moves around Rosie's with braids bouncing, her brown eyes bright. Instead of crying all the time, she goes to Narcotics Anonymous and talks. She knows everyone at Rosie's and jokes with the women; she is a reliably buoyant presence. Beneath her sunny surface, however, Sarah says there lies low self-esteem, degradation, substitution, rationalization. "I have all of those. I'm aware of it. I try to pick myself up and not do the things I've been doing."

For Sarah, most days are spent working in Rosie's clothing room, a volunteer job she has taken on. At one time she worked the conveyor belt in a recycling center. Now she sorts the contents of large plastic bags.

A river of black plastic garbage bags flows into Rosie's. From minivans and station wagons, Jeeps and subcompact cars, the black plastic river pours into the narrow driveway behind the large, red brick building that is Rosie's Place. Almost anything can be found inside these bags: Fisher-Price toys, plastic glasses, a frying pan, blankets. But most of the bags are filled with clothing or shoes—shirts and sweaters, Perry Ellis handbags and belts, slingbacks and Reebok sneakers.

The bags are dropped off just inside the back door, then placed across the hall in large stalls that look as if they might just as easily be home to a cow or a goat. The bags get piled to the ceiling, each crushing the one below. When there's no more room, they are piled along the opposite wall, creating an aisle just wide enough for one person.

It is up to the building staff to unload the bags from the bins, put them on the elevator, and carry them into the clothing room on the second floor. One wall of the room is devoted to shoes. The rest of the room is filled with racks for hanging clothing.

As she works in the clothing room, Sarah watches the ebb and flow of the black plastic bags, a river that never dries up. At times she looks up and groans, knowing there is no way she will get done. Just when the room is finally in order, when everything is on hangers and sorted by size, when she can get down to the subtleties—maybe even start sorting by style—more bags arrive.

Every so often, people have the clothes professionally cleaned before donating them. Sarah always looks for the dry-cleaner bags. "One of the reasons I started working in the clothing room," she says, "was that I got to see what was coming in. I didn't get anything special nobody else got, but I was there, so I just saw it."

~

Adam backs the bus out of the parking lot. "Now you get to see my maneuvering skills!" he says, just as he bumps the bus over the curb, jolting the passengers. They are off on the second leg of the trip.

The drive to the beach takes the Rosie's women past big houses that face the ocean, which is still not visible to them. One huge home with columns on the porch has a statue in the front; another has a fountain and a circular driveway. The women point out the houses they like—trim Dutch Colonials, tidy Capes.

At a large house, someone calls out, "Looks just like home, doesn't it?"

"Yeah, right!" someone else replies.

Eventually Adam makes a turn onto a narrow road with cottages on each side. The beach is getting close. The bus passes a convenience store, but no stops are made there or at the concession stand; no money changes hands all day. For the bus population, everything is provided, even a towel for each woman.

"The Atlantic is on your left," Adam announces over the loudspeaker. "The Pacific's on your right."

He pulls up to a small, sandy parking lot, gated with a padlock. One of the church members who has followed the bus in her car jumps out and opens the gate with her key. As the engine of the parked bus idles loudly, a woman in one of the oceanfront houses walks across her living room and stares out. She moves to be partially hidden behind the drape but continues to peek.

Getting off the bus, the women are enveloped in the heat of the day and stand blinking in the brilliant sunlight. Everything is unloaded. The women carry their own bags and help take out what the church group has put in the storage compartment underneath. Adam gets back in and drives off to park the bus.

In single file from the parking lot, on a path bordered by tall grass, the women carry folding tables, beach chairs, a cooler the size of an enormous trunk, a bright yellow thirty-gallon juice container from McDonald's, boxes of napkins, stacks of cups, and bags of potato chips and cookies. They walk up a small hill. At the top, they see the ocean in front of them and clean sand reaching two hundred yards down to the water where the small rocks and seaweed start. The beach stretches right and left as far as they can see. The landscape is open, as open to sea and sky as the landscape they have left behind is closed in by buildings. The smell of salt is overlaid with a slight fishy odor and coconut oil.

Once on the sand, the women from Rosie's drop the tables, coolers, and urns. They fan out, dotting the beach with chairs and towels. The younger women take care of the older women, who are affectionately and universally called "auntie," helping them across the hot sand and getting them settled.

An elderly man and his wife stare at the group as the women straggle past the couple's blanket. "They've probably never seen so many black women before," one of the church members calls out cheerfully. Two of the guests exchange glowering glances without saying anything.

A lively card game immediately starts on a rummage sale bedspread once the women have settled on the sand. Most of the players never venture toward the water. They laugh, argue, slap down cards—looking up but never stopping when others pause to watch.

Several other women go to test the water, including staffer Julie and intern Julia, and find it numbs their feet immediately. The greenheads—large, stinging flies—are out in force. Adam, who has found a place to park his nonresident bus, also wades out, pant legs rolled up. With his hands on his hips, he walks slowly through the shallow water, stopping now and then to turn his freckled face to the sun, as if wishing to collect solar energy before going back inside the dark bus.

One of the women takes off her dress. Wearing a bra, half slip, and underpants, she wades into the water. Another woman from Rosie's is shocked and stands up, pointing. "She can't go in like that!" But she has.

Sarah Rose, who has been hanging out near the card game, looks up and makes a disapproving face. Pointing out the proximity of two small boys slightly younger than her own, she says, "They won't say nothin', but they'll notice."

~

The philosophy at Rosie's Place is that the women are guests, never clients. The idea comes from the early days when founder Kip Tiernan decided that the women who came to Rosie's should be treated as you would treat guests in your own home. Would guests be expected to serve themselves dinner or wash the dishes? No. If Kip sees someone donate a half-box of dusting powder or a sweater with no buttons, she is irate. "Would you give this as a gift to your sister? No? Then why do you think one of our guests would want it?"

Sarah has found that paying attention to Rosie's philosophy makes her clothing room sorting job easier. If something doesn't look good to her, she tosses it back into the plastic bag. Some of the clothing is out of style, decades out of style, the way she sees it. "But most people give good stuff, though. A lot of people don't even ask for receipts."

Sometimes there are gigantic donations, such as fifteen cases of new white sneakers from a discount store. Those are easy to give away, and most women can wear one of the six sizes. What's harder to find are bras—Sarah would like to see a store or manufacturer donate a large quantity of bras in a variety of styles. That, she thinks, would give the women something they really need when they come in.

Besides sorting and organizing clothes, Sarah assembles household items for women who are setting up apartments. They tell her what they want and she works on pulling it all together. A list from a prospective apartment holder includes everything she would need to move into her own place except furniture, which she can get from the Massachusetts Coalition for the Homeless. "I pick out dishes, pots and pans, bed linens, silverware—everything to set up. I do maybe four household orders a week. I pick out good stuff for them, try to get real nice things. Sometimes I don't have everything all at once, though, so they have to wait."

Sarah doesn't get paid for working in Rosie's clothing room. She is considered a guest/volunteer. She receives some services and a few dollars for expenses from Rosie's, but she also volunteers big chunks of time to "pay back."

Being a guest/volunteer is difficult at times. There is a policy to offer clothing only at posted hours, available to all the women. "If I come through the front way carrying clothes, my friends come up to me and ask me for things. I can't do that! I can't give things to them, because then everybody else comes up and says, 'Why can't you give me something? You gave it to her and I want it, too.'

"I've learned to go up the back stairs," says Sarah, "and not let people see me. They can come to the clothing room, but otherwise it's really awful. They get mad. I feel bad, too, because they're my friends. They think I should help them out—and I want to, but it just gets really hard.

"Sometimes I'll be in the lobby and a woman will just grab something from me. I don't know whether to tell on her. These are my friends. But if I get caught, that's another thing. That's why it's better not to go through the lobby with clothing."

~

Time slows to a standstill. Those who are not playing cards sit in twos and threes on blankets or on folding chairs. Despite the heat, some are bundled up as if heading off a chill March wind. Others stretch out on towels, sleepily catching the sun. The breaking waves create a steady rhythm, loud enough to provide a lulling sound.

An extremely tall, elegant young woman from Rosie's walks over the sand toward the water. She is graceful despite her pregnancy, which seems to be about eight months along. She is wearing a candy-striped maillot suit, and her right breast is escaping from the side. A friend calls to her, "Put your booby back!" She looks down, laughs, and tucks it back in where it belongs.

The church members who carpooled behind the bus get ready to serve lunch. Several of the women from Rosie's help them to put up a folding table, but the table's legs keep collapsing. "How many homeless women does it take to put up a table?" a member of the church asks, trying to be funny.

A woman from Rosie's turns on her. "What do you mean—you're not homeless!"

"You're right. I'm not homeless," the church member admits, putting her hands up like stop signs, essentially saying, "You're right. Say no more, I know I went too far."

In time, the tables are maneuvered into place. Ham-and-cheese sandwiches in plastic bags are brought out, along with chips and the coolers. Those who are hungry, eat.

Because it is the middle of the week, the beach is not crowded. In a scene being played out on miles of beach up and down the Atlantic, a retired couple walks by, hand in hand, and toddlers, closely watched by their mothers, splash in the puddles created by the retreating tide. A Rosie's guest in her seventies sits on a blanket facing the water, with her eyes closed and arms behind her, propping herself up on her elbows. At one point someone offers her a cold drink. She takes the cup and places it beside her but ignores it as she sits peacefully, dazedly, drinking in the sun and breeze.

After an hour and a half, it is time to leave. Hauling trash, tables, and leftover sandwiches, Rosie's women get back on the bus. They return to the church for a cookout—hamburgers and hot dogs cooked on several grills. It is the third meal in about five hours. Several men have appeared at the church to help, along with a bunch of kids.

By now, many of the women from Rosie's Place seem exhausted, out of sorts maybe. One woman talks longingly of needing a shower. Once they get back, those who aren't staying at Rosie's or another shelter in the city will need to take another bus or walk home, carrying their rummage sale goods. No one has asked about today's schedule or how long they'll stay in this suburban community before heading back to the city. Most sit quietly at the tables, knowing that when it's time to go they'll be told.

After everyone has eaten, the hosts circulate, picking up plates after offering seconds. Finally, an announcement is made that the bus is heading back to the city, and everyone starts straggling down the hill to where Adam has parked. The guests thank their hosts. In return, a church member asks if there's anything special they need at Rosie's.

"We could use a sewing machine," Sarah tells her.

"Okay, I'll put an announcement in our church newsletter," the woman promises.

There are lots of hugs. Leaving, one of the guests tells her church host she likes the purple tank top the host is wearing over her bathing suit.

"Here, take it," the woman responds, pulling it over her head.

~

Sarah was sexually assaulted when she was ten years old. "Ten years old! I had no choice," she says. "When I was fourteen, it was my choice. I'm not depressed about that."

For Sarah, the depression, the anger, is there at night. She finds it hard to sleep. Her pattern has become staying up late and sleeping during the day. She is trying to get to know more women, or at least she thinks she should make the attempt. "Men are no problem. I know my motive as to why I want to get to know men. I've been with men my whole life."

When she describes her addiction, she says it is food, booze, and cigarettes. "But," she admits, "a man can be a drug to me, too." She says she does a lot of things she doesn't want to continue. She wants to stop repeating her mistakes, practicing the same behavior and getting the same results. "I'm familiar with the old pain. I want to make new mistakes."

Sarah wants to go back for job training, but she's scared. She has gone to school before, but never when she wasn't using. She is terrified to do this in recovery. She feels the clothing room has helped to keep her out of trouble. "It keeps me from getting too complacent. Man, when I get complacent, I don't do *nothin'*! I just stay at home. That isn't good. This way I feel like I work for my SSI check. I don't know if it's stupid to say that or not. I feel like I need to give to somebody else what God has given to me."

Sarah has worked at a nursing home and at a Veterans Administration hospital. She enjoys working with older people. "It's hard work," she says, "but it gives me a sense of where I should be in my life."

She thinks about going back for training to get two certificates at once, a home health-aide certificate and a nurse's assistant certificate. A lot of people don't want those jobs, she thinks, because they are afraid they will get AIDS. She is not afraid of getting AIDS; she is afraid of going through a training program straight. For her, that's the scary part. "I have potential, I have things I want to do, but the fear gets in the way. Do you know what fear is? Face Everything And Recover.

"Rosie's helps me—it's a learning experience. It doesn't really help me in my recovery, but it gets me with people. A lot of times I don't like people, I want to isolate, I want to run. I'm trying to get to know more women. Some days I work by myself, but most times there are a bunch of interns who get sent up when there's nothing for them to do anywhere else.

"We have fun up in the clothing room, even though we never finish."

2

LILY AND THE LADIES

IT IS THE GLITZIEST AND MOST AMBITIOUS fund-raiser Rosie's Place has ever attempted. "Lunch with Lily and the Ladies" features high-profile Boston women as hosts, and actor/comedian Lily Tomlin as the main attraction. This brainchild of Santa Fareri, Rosie's director of special events, was conceived to raise funds for "A Positive Step," the $1 million-plus capital campaign for the newly opened Rosie's Place house for HIV-positive women. Ten women will find a home in the house, a renovated triple-decker in a working-class Boston neighborhood.

The luncheon is being held at the Park Plaza Castle, the eccentric relative of the classy Park Plaza Hotel. Standing across the street from the hotel, the Park Plaza Castle is an armory-styled, turreted stone structure that looks part Disney World and part Medieval Manor. Even on this glorious Indian-summer day in late October, it is cool, dark, and cavernous inside the building. An occasional stray beam of bright light sneaks in when the door opens.

The ceiling of the main room is two floors up, and the balcony running around the walls is ringed with wrought iron. The room holds an enormous crowd of luncheon guests who are chatting and laughing. Handmade quilts for AIDS victims decorate the walls.

With well-dressed people milling around and a noise level in the upper decibels, it feels like a political rally. There is a huge platform against the wall opposite the exit doors. Large video screens on either side of the platform stand ready to magnify Lily Tomlin and the speakers. Just inside the main entrance door, women sit at tables with thick checklists, holders of the seating assignments.

Though it is billed as Lunch with Lily and the Ladies, Tomlin will appear only as Madame Lupe, the world's oldest beauty expert. The place card has a photo of the guest of honor: Madame Lupe wears a black felt hat with a chartreuse band, and her neck is ringed with rows of pearls of varying sizes. She has applied bright red lipstick by the shovelful and her eyebrows are drawn on with black pencil. Coordinating with nature does not appear to be Madame Lupe's priority.

Boston is not a big celebrity town (when the local press tries the name-drop game, it doesn't last long), but this is a day when female newscasters cluster for a good cause. The major television network affiliates are represented, as are the radio stations. There are some state representatives, a gubernatorial running mate, and the proprietor of the most chichi women's store in the city. Serious rubber-necking is going on among the luncheon guests.

Actor/comedian Rosie O'Donnell steps out of a limousine at the main entrance. Outwardly, she is an unremarkable guest, casually dressed in jeans, a white sweatshirt, and a denim jacket. A spiffed-up woman with a henna pageboy hustles over and gushes, "I loved you in your new movie, Rosie." O'Donnell twirls around to face her and says, "You did? You were one of two people! Everyone hated it!" She laughs.

O'Donnell passes through a line of unofficial greeters from the Massachusetts Democratic Party who are handing out campaign buttons for local candidates she doesn't recognize. She pauses for a moment and then reaches across, picks up a Kennedy for Senator pin, and walks the few steps to the door.

Inside there are more than one hundred tables for ten, and at each place setting there is a large white box tied with a bow. As the guests start sitting down, they eye the boxes. Are they door prizes? No, they are lunch. Tickets to the event may cost a hundred dollars per person, but the box lunch is designed to keep serving expenses down. It is an elegant box lunch to be sure—gourmet chicken-and-eggplant sandwiches; bottles of spring water and thermoses of coffee are on each table.

Evelyn Murphy—Democratic party stalwart and former state Lieutenant Governor—is the first speaker. She reminds the luncheon-goers that Rosie's was the first emergency shelter in the United States specifically for women. At Rosie's, she says, a woman can get tutoring and find help in earning her General

Equivalency Diploma (GED). She can even find, free of charge, suitable clothes for interviews or other needs. Murphy goes on to say that Rosie's newest project is also a trail-blazing endeavor. A Positive Step will provide a home for HIV-positive women, the first home some of the women have ever had. "We've shown we're interested in justice, not charity, for women, regardless of their situation," Murphy says.

Co-chair Victoria Kennedy—wife of the senior senator from Massachusetts—bounds up the steps to join Murphy on stage. Slim, with cascading dark hair, Victoria Kennedy wears a Kennedy button and a red AIDS awareness ribbon on her blue suit. Her husband is in a tight race for reelection (which he will win the following week). "AIDS is on the rise," she notes, "and women of color are most seriously affected. A large number of them are fleeing domestic violence and abuse."

Cheers greet Kip Tiernan as she comes up onto the stage. She is wearing a magenta turtleneck, a navy blue jacket, khaki pants, and a gray tweed hat. "They told me no one would recognize me without the hat," she tells the crowd.

"You all know Rosie's Place. We're the gang that's been comforting the afflicted and occasionally afflicting the comfortable for years," Kip points out from under her hat. "Years from now, when historians ask, 'When did the women's movement resurface, anyway?' all of you can proudly say, 'Today, when we all took a positive step with Rosie's Place.' Because you all came through these doors, you took a positive step toward making visible what has been called the invisible epidemic."

Kip tells of the organization's refusal to take public funding. "That's why we've been able to stay unbought, unowned, and unpaid for by anyone except the general public, to whom we owe a profound thanks," she says. She speaks of how Rosie's has been housing homeless women with HIV for more than three years. "Our financial independence is key to offering women what they need for decent lives. They need permanent housing and care. Most of all they need justice, not charity."

Her heroes, Kip goes on to say, are the women who come to Rosie's Place, the staff members who keep them on track, and the donors who support Rosie's, including the people in attendance. One local hero, Kip points out, is "Frugal Fannie, sometimes known as Kathleen Doxer, whose retail warehouse is giving formerly homeless guests the chance to have careers, not just jobs."

~

In conversation, Kathleen Doxer will say, "I've had a really messed-up life. I'm a hard worker, always have been, and I do not have much admiration for people who don't work hard. I know how much women want to work."

Kathleen started working at a dry cleaner when she was twelve years old. She was there for three hours after school every day and all day Saturdays through high school. "I was the fourth of six kids in the family, and I had to pay for my own lunch and other expenses," she says.

Kathleen knew her family would not help her go to college. If anyone in her Irish Catholic family was to go, it would be one of the boys. Still, by living at home and working part-time, she managed to go to art school for one year after high school. During that year, she became pregnant.

"My mother was so bullshit she wouldn't talk to me. She said I ruined her tombstone. She was planning to have it say, 'All my daughters were virtuous and all my sons were brave.' And now she couldn't have it on her goddamn tombstone. Isn't that pitiful?"

There seemed to be only one solution. At eighteen Kathleen got married. "I was a mother with no life. Most of my friends were in college and leading what I thought were exciting lives. This was the late sixties—everyone was traipsing around in vans all over the place."

Kathleen had a daughter, then another daughter. She and her husband bought a house in a small town thirty miles west of Boston, not far from where she had grown up. She worked first in a convenience store and then in a grocery store. After paying for day care, she made a dollar an hour, but she and her husband needed it to help pay the mortgage. In time, as the women's movement came to the forefront, she came to feel she wasn't doing anything worthwhile.

She had been working in the supermarket for a couple of years when another cashier, who had been there less time, was promoted to the courtesy booth. Something snapped inside Kathleen. She didn't go into work the next day.

"It was bad enough I was killing myself, not making any money, and now they were going to take away my self-esteem? So I was unemployed. I went up to the welfare office, and I applied for food stamps and got them. All of a sudden, there I am, getting money from the state. I wondered why I had been killing myself working all those years. That felt good, to take back for a little while."

When Kathleen's husband, who was a truck driver, lost his job, she began to look for a new way to earn money. She had always liked to sew, to make clothes. She bought a few bolts of fabric and started putting together women's pocketbooks. "I sold them for twenty-five dollars to gift shops and anyone else who would buy them, but we still weren't making any real money."

Around that time, Kathleen was called to school for a parent-teacher conference. Ruth Mack, the school's guidance counselor, wanted to talk about some behavioral problems with Kathleen's first-grader. "I went in and I had this bravura about me, thinking no one is going to tell me my kid is screwed up. So I went in, sat down, and she said, 'Kathleen, what is going on with you?' "

Kathleen found herself telling Ruth how she felt she wasn't doing anything with her life. "I thought I was a nothing, with no opinion, no voice. I wanted to be something. I felt really bad because I knew my daughter needed her mother."

Ruth pointed out that Kathleen needed a mother herself. She had started working at an early age, and she had started a family before she had a chance to develop her interest in art or to enjoy life on her own. It was a revelation to Kathleen. "I sound so stupid and naive that that could be an awakening! Here I was, a twenty-six-year-old woman, and I needed my mother?"

They talked about Kathleen's interest in art—about how her education had been cut short, how she had lost sight of using that talent and doing something with her life. Finally, as she was leaving, Ruth said to her, "Now, Kathleen, what do you really want now?"

"And I said, 'I want to have the kind of job that when I walk into a building, people respect me. I want a job where I am somebody. When I pull up in my car and I walk in, I want to feel that I'm important.' "

Looking back, Kathleen thinks that it was probably the first conversation that ever really got through to her. "It was a very odd time. You know how you go through your life pretending and acting? I sat down with Ruth and it didn't have to be an act. She cut through it all when she made me think about what I wanted to do—it got to my heart."

When Ruth asked what that job was, Kathleen told her she didn't know where it was or if it even existed. It was their first and only conversation, but it changed the direction of her life. "At that point," Kathleen says, "I had been willing to take from the system, to go get my food stamps." She stops for a moment and then continues, "Every successful woman can look back and see how someone, somewhere gave her encouragement, a break. In this case, a school guidance counselor was the person who told me I could have something. It was the first time I had ever heard that."

About two weeks later Kathleen got a call from someone who knew of her art background, asking her if she could do some advertising work for a local store. "I lied," remembers Kathleen. "I said I could do anything. I told them I had graduated from art school, that I had clients, that I had an art studio. I just lied my way in and got the job."

She threw herself into her work. After working at a dry cleaner, after being a cashier, after being on food stamps, she wanted to work at what she was good at, to use her artistic talent. "I was doing well with this company. For the first time I liked what I was doing. I liked myself."

As her career developed, however, her marriage dissolved. Eventually, she and her husband divorced.

Now she was a single mother, working to make her career go. The end of the marriage was a beginning. "I felt as if God had given me a second chance."

Her work paid off. After a few years, she and Orrin Doxer, who would become her second husband, took a conventional clothing store and grew it into Frugal Fannie's, which represented a new concept in merchandising. Frugal Fannie's is geared to the working woman who has limited time to shop and is interested in buying quality clothing at reasonable prices. There are now six Frugal Fannie's chain stores—three in suburban Boston. All six are in industrial park warehouses, open just on weekends, with a no-frills atmosphere and plenty of parking.

Kathleen is in charge of advertising, store image, and design. "I know it doesn't look like much design is going on," she says, referring to the bare-bones look of the warehouses, "but there is. I do all the radio ads, TV spots, and newspaper ads. I do all the internal communications, the corporate communications, and the in-house newsletter."

The Doxers have sponsored a number of major benefits, including the Share Your Heart annual Valentine's benefit, Lunch with Lily and the Ladies, and a seventieth birthday party for Kip Tiernan. The Doxers' association with Rosie's first began in 1989 as the recession came into full bloom and homelessness became more visible. In a women-helping-women effort, Frugal Fannie's offered to donate used coats to

Rosie's, and a coat trade-in began at the store. When a woman came into Frugal Fannie's to buy a coat, she would be given ten dollars off if she turned in an old coat. The old coat was taken to a tailor if it needed repair, then dry cleaned, poly bagged, and delivered to Rosie's clothing room.

"We didn't want to deliver the coats in big plastic trash bags, all rolled up in a ball or without buttons," says Kathleen. "We wanted the women to be able to go to a clothing room and to shop, selecting the size and color off a rack like in a store. We saw how it could be done in a dignified way."

The coat program took off and proved to be good for business. Kathleen asked Kip whether Frugal's could publicize its involvement with Rosie's. Kathleen knew that the name *Rosie's Place* had an instant and positive recognition factor. She felt their customers responded to and were touched by the connection. She assured Kip the publicity would be tastefully done, and the store would let Kip see anything mentioning Rosie's before it was run. Kip agreed.

While Frugal Fannie's donations and underwritings have been significant, it is Kathleen Doxer's internships that bring real joy to Kip. In 1994, Kathleen implemented a plan for one-year paid internships for two women from Rosie's Place. During the year, the women would learn about the organization from the inside by rotating through the various departments. At the end of the year, they would be guaranteed jobs at the store's corporate offices. "You can't change everybody's life," comments Kathleen, "but if you can give one person an opportunity, she can change her own life."

As the internship program evolved, Kathleen took a hard look at the total cost. She was surprised at the large sum of money required to run the program, and she wondered if, from the standpoint of Rosie's, it was the best use of the funding. She went back to Kip and asked if Kip wouldn't rather have Frugal Fannie's simply write a check. Kip wanted the program.

"That's how much it meant to her to get the women out of there," Kathleen says. "This internship program is tackling problems of low self-esteem and low self-image."

~

One of the first interns was Leslie Ross, who arrived at Rosie's Place when a friend asked her if she wanted to have lunch at the Ritz. Knowing the Ritz part was a joke but knowing nothing else, Leslie was surprised by what she found. "Rosie's was really clean. There were flowers on the tables, and there was a piano player. It was cheerful. The volunteers treated me like a woman, like a person. I'd been to other shelters and some of them make you feel down. This one made me feel alive."

Leslie was the fourth of eight children raised by a single mother. Her family had moved to one of the

Boston housing projects after they had lost their home in a fire when she was a teenager.

In her thirties and with a grown son, Leslie finished high school and worked in a series of clerical jobs that each lasted just a few months. She was approached by Rosie's advocate Julie Mason to do the Frugal Fannie's internship. Leslie was apprehensive about making a commitment to a year-long program where the expectations were so high. "Julie pushed me to take that step."

From sleeping on a day bed in a sheeted-off portion of her mother's living room, Leslie moved into an apartment in the suburbs near Frugal's. "Rosie's set me up with everything I needed: furniture, dishes, a microwave."

Kathleen sent her to a twelve-week Dale Carnegie course that coached her in public speaking and problem solving. Leslie had been self-conscious about her speech ever since she had had to repeat second grade because school authorities thought she talked too fast.

When Leslie began at Frugal Fannie's, Kathleen gave her and the program's other intern a clothing allowance of one thousand dollars so they would feel comfortable with the other staff members. Kathleen thought she was doing them "a terrific favor" when she also gave them the services of a professional personal shopper who had worked with many newscasters and executive women in Boston. Every woman, the personal shopper believed, should have a navy blazer and gray flannel skirt. There was no way the interns wanted either of these things, but they were so grateful to get help—any help at all—they didn't protest.

Kathleen knew there was a problem with the clothes. "Leslie very often wears her hair up in extension braids and exotic earrings—she's a very savvy dresser. But sometimes she'd be wearing an outfit that just wasn't her. I could tell it was someone else's taste thrust on her." By the time Kathleen realized what was going on, however, the allowance had been spent.

When the fall season arrived, there was another thousand-dollar clothing allowance. This time there was no personal shopper. The interns joined other Frugal Fannie's staff members when the store was open for employees only. They picked out what they wanted, and this time the clothes reflected their own style.

As a part of her internship, Leslie had to go back to Rosie's Place and talk about the FANS program, an acronym for Female Achievers Need Support. Frugal Fannie's is not the only sponsor in the FANS program, but it was the first. The older guests at Rosie's were generally supportive of what Leslie was doing. Some of the younger women, however, were critical. One woman told Leslie that she no longer spoke like a black woman.

Kathleen thinks it meant a lot to Leslie to get dressed up for work every day in a blazer and skirt (even a navy blazer and a gray flannel skirt) and to sit at a desk. "When we were crafting this program for the women," explains Kathleen, "we didn't want them to feel that they were just working in a service. It's tricky because we're in a retail business and so most of our jobs are in a store, working with customers. But we wanted the interns to feel they were learning something and being given the opportunity to contribute and use their brains. I think that's the key to getting their self-esteem on track for the first time."

As an intern in the accounting department, Leslie was given figures to analyze. For the first time in her life, she could use her brain on the job, and the people around her had the courtesy to give her the time to do so. "While Leslie was in our accounting department, she came up with a way of tracking outstanding checks. We're a $53 million company, and we never did it until she developed it," Kathleen says.

Leslie feels she went from one home—at Rosie's—to another at Frugal Fannie's. During her internship, she found someone to emulate in every department. She particularly liked the professionalism of the accounting department. There she found a strong, positive woman as a role model. It was an important part of her experience. Now she works in the advertising department, using the desktop publishing equipment to lay out company publications and to design signs.

Whether the company's task at hand is reviewing accounting procedures or previewing models for television advertising, Kathleen wants the opinions of the interns. She feels it is part of the process and good for the organization. One time, one of the interns was afraid to speak up. "It was so ingrained in her that she was not important, that she should keep her mouth shut—especially in the field of business—how could she ever think she had an opinion that counted? And, along with everything else," Kathleen continues, "I want their opinions as black women—that in particular is important to me. In our organization we have this whole teamwork thing. Everyone speaks up. Everyone."

~

Kip introduces some other heroes. One is Mary Fisher, who in 1991 tested positive for HIV and went on to found the Family AIDS Network. A former staff assistant to President Ford, Fisher stepped into the limelight at the Republican National Convention in 1992. The epidemic nature of AIDS was just becoming known to the country as a whole. In her speech to the convention, Fisher emphasized there was no place in America that was safe from the risk of AIDS—no race or religion, no family or community. According to Kip, Fisher's going public in a time of cynicism, fear, ignorance, and hostility made her a hero. "Guts, passion, truth, grace—that's my kind of hero."

Mary Fisher comes onto the stage. Small, pretty, and blonde, she points out that HIV asks only one thing of those it may attack: "Are you human?"

Fisher tells how she was first introduced to the Rosie's Place community as a photographer working on a project about caregivers. When she arrived at the Rosie's residence where women with HIV were staying, a woman named Charlotte was in the final stages of AIDS. Fisher listened quietly as Charlotte discussed her own death with the manager at her bedside.

"Charlotte wanted to be where she could hold her children. She wanted to die at home," Fisher explains to the luncheon guests. Charlotte felt more at home at Rosie's than any place she had been before.

Fisher speaks of how women are present at birth by biology and at death by sociology. "Part of what made our mothers and our sisters strong was the ability to see death. A growing network cannot deny death. By accepting death in the lives of the AIDS community, we gain strength.

"Some neighbors think zoning laws will protect them," she says, referring to the avoidance of people with AIDS. "They think of A Positive Step as a house of death. We know better—it is stuffed with gifts, a home of love."

Death will find us all, Fisher reminds the audience, but it does not need to defeat us. "You're giving to the AIDS community." Though Charlotte is gone, Fisher goes on to say, the courage she brought to the house has lived after her in the form of the smiles, zest, and commitment of those still there.

"Seeing Rosie O'Donnell here today makes me think it wasn't a random choice of names—*Rosie's*—for Rosie's Place is just as full of spunk and sass, where the memory of abuse gives way to laughter. It is where gentle affection fills the night. . . . It is full of grace and peace," concludes Fisher, "a place not only to say good-bye but thank you."

~

The much-anticipated Madame Lupe slinks onto the stage, decked out as advertised, a vision in green and black. "I see that my reputation precedes me," she coos. "Good afternoon, dear ones. I am Madame Lupe, the world's oldest living beauty expert. My family, the Lupes, have been innovators in the beauty business." Madame Lupe tells how her grandmother landed on Plymouth Rock and opened the first beauty parlor. As "the Mary Kay of her day," Madame Lupe's grandmother fought for the freedom for women to wear makeup in church. She was run out of town in her wedgies.

Madame Lupe goes on to say the world is divided into only two groups: People who have cellulite and people who are cellulite. "Gravity is an evil force; fight the enemy with ambiance," she advises. "Avoid excessive emotion. Joy and pain, while part of the human experience, will leave an imprint on the face like a waffle iron. Repeat this each day: 'Lines, lines so reprehensible / Go have a field day with Victoria Principal.' "

Mugging and throwing off one-liners, Tomlin has clearly found an impressive addition to her family of characters. (Ernestine the telephone operator will appear at next year's luncheon.) While Madame Lupe provokes waves of laughter throughout the room, strangers sitting together at tables introduce themselves, joined by their donations of one hundred dollars for box lunches and three hours during the week to support Rosie's campaign. The luncheon is, in many respects, exhilarating for this generally feel-good crowd, but it is set against a deadly serious backdrop, for no one can forget why they are there. The women who will benefit from the Positive Step campaign are battling the many problems of poverty as well as their latest hurdle, AIDS.

How Lily Tomlin came to be involved with Rosie's Place is a story worthy of Madame Lupe herself. In 1984, just as Rosie's was marking its tenth year, a devastating fire threatened to close it. Tomlin was in town for her one-woman show, "Search for Signs of Intelligent Life in the Universe." Knowing Tomlin's reputation as a supporter of poor women, Kip sought her out, and according to Kip, another hero emerged for Rosie's. Tomlin jumped in with a check for fifteen thousand dollars.

Together with her writer, Jane Wagner, Tomlin helps to show the women of Rosie's Place how art provides the gift of truth. "The Tomlin/Wagner hallmark," Kip tells the audience, "is the conviction that we have some power to alter the course of our world, as well as our own lives, if we are willing to care enough."

A last speaker comes to the lectern: Rosie's Place Executive Director Julie Brandlen. "I have known women who have been brutally beaten and women who have died a slow, casual, invisible death from loneliness. Charlotte said, 'I have been looking for love all my life, and I found it at Rosie's Place.' Our work," concludes Julie, "is being present with our sisters."

After the luncheon, Kathleen Doxer looks at the list of attendees and whispers, "I can't believe it." The guest list for the luncheon includes a name she hasn't seen or heard for twenty years: Ruth Mack.

3

FRIDAY LUNCH

GEORGE KEADY PULLS HIS FADED maroon sedan up to Rosie's Place early on a Friday morning and walks stiffly to the door. George is a big man in his seventies, with sparkling blue eyes and bushy white hair. After working late the night before at his "real" (i.e., paying) job, he has had to get up early for his weekly volunteer stint in Rosie's kitchen. The street is almost deserted. Two women pull a shopping cart with a baby in the basket. They recognize George from down the block and wave to him.

George then greets the staffer who opens the door for him. "Hello, dear!" He's a little breathless from the effort of walking the fifty feet from his parking space to the door. "How are ya?" While his face may be from Ireland, George's speech leaves no doubt that he has lived in a Boston neighborhood all his life. He refers to himself as "one of the poor boys from Brighton," a small piece of Boston south of the Charles River, sandwiched between Brookline and Newton.

Going directly to the kitchen, George finds he has the place to himself and heads for the storage room in the back. He hauls a box of onions off the top of a stack of boxes beside the produce refrigerator and totes it to the big counter in the kitchen. He dumps out ten onions the size of grapefruits and goes to work, chopping through the pale layers with the air of someone who has spent years just cutting up onions. Altogether, he probably has. Unlike everyone else who works in the kitchen and whose training has been on-the-job at best, George is a professional. Starting in the U.S. Navy, he has cooked steadily for decades. Quantities don't faze him; he has overseen as many as 2500 dinners a night at some of the mammoth chateau-type restaurants that used to be scattered around Boston.

With only about a hundred lunch customers and a single menu, being the top chef at Rosie's is one of George's easiest jobs. It also pays the least, since George is a volunteer. He cooks the food America lived on in the 1940s and '50s. Vegetables have sticks of butter mixed into them. Red meat is frequently on the menu. Fish comes with lemon sauce, broccoli is covered with cheese, and chicken dishes are invariably creamy. The food reminds many of Rosie's guests of how things used to be.

~

Beverly Strasnick is responsible for supplying Rosie's Place with four of the pool of volunteers from the patent-law firm of Wolf, Greenfield & Sacks every Friday. The relationship started a few years ago, when Pia Zonne, the Rosie's volunteer coordinator who was responsible for building the volunteer effort into the several-hundred-person force it is now, did one presentation after another. Pia talked about the organization, the philosophy behind it, and the commitment required, and she signed up volunteers on the spot. Beverly, a legal assistant to one of the partners, was later drafted as the liaison between Wolf, Greenfield & Sacks and Rosie's.

Beverly is a take-no-prisoners kind of leader. She makes sure the volunteers get to Rosie's and whips them into shape in the kitchen once they are there. Before becoming liaison, Beverly had helped out at charity events for other places; she had donated bags of clothes and she had written checks when asked, but she had never before done direct service with the poor. Members of Wolf, Greenfield & Sacks are typically timid about going to Rosie's as volunteers the first time. At Rosie's, Wolf, Greenfield & Sacks is known simply as the Firm. It may be a short geographic trip to Rosie's from the Firm, but given the Firm's million-dollar view of the city and Boston Harbor up on the seventeenth, eighteenth, and nineteenth floors, it is a long demographic leap.

Volunteers from the Firm think Rosie's Place may be a rough place, and they don't know what they will find there. Many of them have never been to Rosie's neighborhood, which is primarily poor and industrial. Its location is intimidating to some. Beverly says, however, that so far, every person who has come to Rosie's once has asked to be put on the permanent schedule.

This does not mean it is always easy to get people to go to Rosie's. Beverly sends e-mail or visits potential volunteers in their offices, and she uses a variety of tactics ranging from guilt-tripping to strong-arming, whatever works. "Please don't tell me you can't spare three hours a month! You go to lunch for longer than that every day," she tells them, only partly in jest.

Beverly is on the schedule for one Friday a month, but she ends up at Rosie's more often, sometimes three Fridays in a month because everyone switches around. She sends out reminders the day before, but there are always problems, always excuses. "What do you mean?" she says to an employee who has just told Beverly that her boss can't spare her at lunchtime. "Don't tell me that. You're on the calendar—this is your Friday. I don't care how busy you are, you are going to be there!"

Beverly does understand how hard it is for people to get away on a busy Friday. "I know major things come up. Sometimes it looks like nobody is going to show up, but some of us always do. It's hard for people to do it, especially at the end of the week. It is a sizable commitment on the part of the Firm, because they pay people when they're at Rosie's, and when you talk about partners being there for fifteen or eighteen hours a month, that's a sizable amount of money," she says. Wolf, Greenfield & Sacks is the only corporate group to send volunteers to Rosie's Place every week.

When Beverly walks into Rosie's, she grabs an apron out of the linen drawer and looks around to refresh all the supplies. She makes sure plastic knives, forks, and spoons are in the large, round cups and paper napkins are in the dispensers. She watches for ways to make the kitchen run more efficiently. The staff is usually happy to take suggestions from the volunteers, such as reorganizing a drawer so that forks can be replaced quickly if there are not enough in the course of lunch.

Because the dinner plates are donated and come in all sizes, Beverly sorts them by size before the serving begins. "I don't want to make one woman think she's getting less than someone else sitting at the same table just because her plate is bigger and the food looks skimpy," Beverly explains. "Some of those plates are more like salad plates, and others are as big as platters."

A Rosie's staff member oversees the general lunch operation, supervising the volunteer workforce and assigning jobs, but George organizes the strategy of getting the food prepared and ready to serve exactly at noon. Because of recent heart trouble, he has needed more helpers than he is used to. Delegation comes hard to him—George has spent his adult life grabbing pans out of the oven and putting them where they need to go. It is not easy for him to ask a volunteer to help with the heavy lifting.

The volunteers all seem to find their own niches after a few shifts. They gravitate to what they like to do or simply stay away from certain jobs. One member of the Firm has become George's unofficial *sous* chef, learning the business at his side. George, who has never been married, takes on an almost fatherly role toward his young helper.

"Just pour the lemonade in here," George tells his apprentice, who is looking skeptically at the unusual sauce. George continues to shovel several pounds of green beans into the stainless steel pan. "Mix 'em up real good . . . there, that's it."

~

Twelve meals are served at Rosie's every week: lunch and dinner Monday through Friday and dinner on weekends. There are no prerequisites for being served. Any woman is welcome to come and to bring her children with her, as long as they are not missing school to be there. No men are allowed except as volunteer workers. At lunch, the dining room is full of women, some with babies and small youngsters.

Near the dining room is the drop-in advocacy office, the place where women go for help with a variety of needs: housing, legal assistance, medical care, emergency groceries. Twice a month during Friday lunch, an ophthalmologist arrives with a group of students to perform eye exams in the adjoining television room. Hundreds of pairs of eyeglasses have been donated to fill the women's prescriptions.

It is in the dining room, the only really large space at Rosie's, that groups congregate. Up to about 120 women can be seated comfortably there at one time. When a staff meeting, a party, a performance, or any large meeting is planned, the dining room is where it will happen. Sooner or later, almost everyone working at Rosie's Place stops by the dining room during a lunch.

The room has a worn linoleum floor. Its walls are painted a nondescript cream, broken up with black-and-white photos of guests and volunteers. A picture of a beaming Kip Tiernan faces the kitchen from across the room. There are fresh flowers on each table, and plants and other decorations in the room vary according to the season. Sliding doors from the dining room lead outside to a large, fenced-in patio with a couple of picnic tables, a terraced, grassy area, and a vegetable garden in the summer.

There are two ice machines in the dining room, one of which is temperamental. Today it is taking the day off. "It's a typical Rosie's appliance," a staff member says, shrugging her shoulders after attempting to get some ice into her glass and getting instead a glass of water. "Sometimes it works and sometimes it doesn't."

The whole kitchen is open to the dining room. There are more than thirty volunteer groups, which

Rosie's calls caterers, that provide full meals in large coolers or stacks of pans every month. Once every couple of months a caterer brings in gourmet sandwiches and a salad, and George gets the Friday off. Other prepared food comes from Second Helpings, which drops off soups, stews, and casseroles from restaurants in the city. Otherwise the meal preparation is done right at Rosie's. Much of the food that is prepared at Rosie's comes out of the food budget, as do staple ingredients such as milk, butter, eggs, bread, and cheese. Food is purchased in bulk from the Boston Food Bank, a bargain at fourteen cents per pound.

At 11:30 the doors to the dining room open and the women come in. The size of the dining crowd varies—small at the beginning of the month and large at the end, when welfare money is running out. The policy is to serve a meal to whomever comes, which sometimes means the staff person on duty must send volunteers scrambling in the pantry for more food at the last minute. Some of the women entering the room have come to the side door at Rosie's Place early in the morning. A staff member has let them into the lobby, where they wait until the doors open for lunch.

A few of the Rosie's guests go immediately to a table to drop their things, but many stop to pick up a bowl of soup that is being served by Agnes Cahill just inside the dining room door. Guests can come up for soup as many times as they like, and they get crackers or slices of bread to go with it. In the wintertime the Friday lunch crowd goes through gallons of soup or chowder.

In her bright red apron, "Aggie" is a mainstay of the Friday volunteer staff. This small, lively woman has been giving her time to Rosie's Place every week for more than ten years. Retired from the fashion industry in Boston, she sometimes brings out-of-town guests with her and puts them to work. Several years ago, when she was chairman of the board and the director's job was waiting to be filled, Aggie served for a few months as executive director of Rosie's Place.

The soup of the day may be anything, except on Fridays, when it is always "The Firm Soup." The tradition started one Friday when someone asked George to describe the soup—that day a concoction of a little bit of everything left over in the refrigerator, primarily leftover beef, leftover corn, and leftover gravy. While tasty, it defied even the most creative naming talents, so George simply called it the Firm Soup. He still makes it himself and serves it every week, and every week the ingredients change.

After the soup stop, Rosie's guests typically line up at the long counter that separates the dining room from the kitchen area. The staff person in charge gets the openers out, or instructs volunteers in getting them ready. Openers are the second lunch course. They may be small plates or bowls of leftover pasta salad, cut-up sandwiches, or cheese and crackers.

Most often, they are plates of fruit or vegetables. A move toward organic produce has been a tough sell, a change that is greeted with skepticism by some of the guests. One guest picks up a small plate with apple slices, a bunch of grapes, and a banana. "I am not eating *that,*" she says, eyeing the rather brownish banana. She slides it onto another plate on the counter, trading it for more grapes.

There may not be enough of one thing to serve the entire dining room, so openers may vary. When the guests have taken everything off the counter, it is usually noon and time for the rest of lunch to be served. The women get their own drinks at the beverage station—there is coffee, hot water for tea or Sanka, milk, and a choice of two kinds of juice. They pick up their own plastic forks, knives, spoons, and napkins. After that, they select a table and wait to be served. The tables are round and Formica-topped. The chairs around them are metal stacking chairs with thick vinyl backs and seats. Most of the vinyl is split and the foam is showing. Despite the appearance of the furniture, Rosie's guests are treated as guests—they are served their meals on china. The volunteers dish out the food at the counter, carry trays, act as "spotters"—food deliverers—for the day, and wash dishes.

Friday lunch is like no other meal at Rosie's. George is a congenial host, a much-appreciated cook, and part of a gender shift that adds a different flavor to the atmosphere. Safe men are in short supply in many of these women's lives. Thus, George and the men from the Firm bring a lightness to the dining room that changes the atmosphere slightly during this last lunch of the week.

Another man who contributes to the lightness is Jack MacIsaac, the only man to bring music to Rosie's on a regular basis. He is George's shadow, an older man in a cap and glasses who sometimes drives in with George but usually trails in later, warming up just as the doors open for the women. He plays for an hour on the well-worn piano in the far corner of the dining room. For years the volunteer coordinator tried to get someone from one of the music schools in Boston to come into Rosie's to play. It never worked. Eventually it was self-taught Jack who came and stayed.

"Turn off the radio," he says in a low whisper to Aggie, who is standing by the boombox, soup ladle in hand. She turns it off quickly as he heads over to begin playing.

~

If Rosie's ran a popularity contest for volunteers, George would likely win. He greets Rosie's guests when they come in, and he keeps the conversation going throughout lunch, back and forth from the open kitchen area to the tables. Even so, lunch would not work without the other volunteers who keep things moving.

Beverly is in charge of helping George with the main course today. She sets up the assembly line and stacks the plates. She works with George to judge the size of the crowd and to determine serving sizes based on the amount of food available. She checks out the quantity of potatoes and green beans and then has a one-minute meeting with George to talk about portion control. After that she shows volunteers how much to put on the plate.

Members of the Firm line up to form an assembly line: The first person slides Salisbury steak onto the plate and hands it over for green beans. The second person dishes out the appropriate portion of beans with a slotted spoon. The final member of the line scoops up mashed potatoes and ladles on the gravy. When there are six plates on a tray, a server picks up the tray and goes out into the dining room.

It is the spotter's job to remove the plates from the tray, putting one down in front of each person who wants a lunch. The spotter has to make sure that each guest gets a plate and that no guest gets more than one until everyone is served. After that, if there is enough food, seconds are offered.

Today the spotter is wearing a bright red shirt—she's easy for each server to find as she moves from table to table, not missing anyone. Each guest is supposed to be seated at a table to get a plate. The spotter also counts the number of guests as she goes through the dining room.

One woman, sitting alone at a table, is slumped over, dozing with her head on the table. The spotter quietly puts a plate next to her and then moves on to the next table where the occupants are awake.

"Hey, I don't want any of those beans!" says one guest, shoving the plate back against the spotter before it touches the table.

"Would you get me a plate without beans on it when you go back," the spotter says quietly to the server. In this case, the server delivers the plate directly to the guest, minus beans.

Though any woman is welcome to come by for lunch at Rosie's, many of the same women come every day. Some have been coming for years. Some of them live in low-income apartments in the neighborhood; others are in the shelter system, staying at different places overnight; and some have no regular place to live. Many of the women know each other, at least by sight. There are sisters who live apart but who come to have lunch together. There is a young woman who comes in with a tiny, bundled-up baby. A staff member takes the infant on a tour of the dining room while the young woman eats lunch. As anywhere else, there are mothers pushing their reluctant children to eat—at Rosie's, this may be the last chance for several hours to get food into them.

In one corner of the room is the kids' area, with toys, small tables, and children's books in bookcases. Babies sit in their mothers' laps or in highchairs pulled over from where they are stored against the wall. Children can go up to the main counter and request paper and crayons, which are kept in a kitchen drawer. Their drawings are stuck up in the kitchen.

"No lunch," a tiny girl in pigtails tells the spotter as she jumps up from her chair in the children's area. "I don't like that."

"Give her a plate," her mother says, balancing a small baby in her lap as she tries to get her daughter to sit down.

At one table there are two women and five children. The women are one of the mother-daughter pairs who come to Rosie's, sometimes bringing their young children. The generations leapfrog. The mother has children ranging from age ten to age twenty, and her daughter, the twenty year old, has two small children of her own.

"Hey, you change the diaper—you're the mother," the woman says to her daughter, chiding her just a little.

One of the guests is the unofficial St. Francis of the dining room. Any day of the year, even in blowing rain or snow, she opens the sliding doors to the patio and sprinkles whatever bread she has been able to collect. Beverly made a friend when she started saving day-old pieces of bread for the growing flock of birds. Beverly says, "She will take half the bread that's intended for the whole dining room—I've seen her do it. A lot of the women resent this, of course; she is taking food out of their mouths. So I try to put the ends and broken pieces from about fifteen loaves for her in a bag. That's a lot of bread!"

Prior to coming to Rosie's Place, Beverly says, members of the Firm invariably think of it in stereotypes. They envision a soup kitchen, an operation resembling that in the television show "M*A*S*H*," with long tables and servers slopping unidentifiable meat on each person's plate. They are usually surprised to see women served lunch on china plates at tables with vases of fresh flowers.

There is typically plenty of food at Rosie's, often enough for seconds for those who want to come up and fill their plates again after everyone has been served. When George is cooking, the women count on generous helpings of rich food with no regard to fat content. It is hard to tell where the food itself leaves off and the nourishing atmosphere he creates begins, but the experience for many of the women seems to be one that is a natural, end-of-the-week mood elevator.

The comfort aspect of George's lunches is apparently not limited to the regular diners at Rosie's. A Unitarian student minister visiting Chicago and Boston for two months from Transylvania came to work the lunch shift at Rosie's one Friday. She proclaimed George's pork chop suey "the best meal I've had in the States."

Many of the women do not come to socialize; they don't even pay much attention to what they are eating. Some are clearly looking for a comfortable place to be left alone. They may be exhausted, hung over, sick, struggling with an addiction. The policy is to treat them respectfully. Staff members are supposed to give them an opportunity to get help but not to force anything on them.

Other women are looking for a fight. The staff member at the door tries to spot problems and to weed out women who are acting unpredictable or abusive. Abuse, whether it is verbal or physical, is not tolerated. If there is an occurrence in the dining room, a staff member talks to the women involved and gets it settled, which may mean asking a woman to leave or barring her from Rosie's for a certain length of time.

Over the years, clear guidelines have been set up. Staff members are posted at the doors to monitor who is coming in and to make sure nothing is going out—flower vases or highchairs, for example.

If there are enough volunteers, one person is assigned to handing out items from the drawers behind the main counter. The drawers are stocked with various items: packets of instant decaffeinated coffee, tea bags, and artificial sweeteners; turquoise books of matches and silver cardboard ashtrays; tampons and sanitary napkins; three styles of condoms. The drawer that attracts the most interest, however, is what is known as the "hygiene drawer," which houses a collection of soaps and shampoos free for the asking. If there is anything in the hygiene drawer, a handful of women can turn into something resembling a stampede. Friends of Rosie's have learned to collect small, sample-size bottles for the hygiene drawer.

"Got any perfume?" one guest says, coming up and looking in as the drawer is opened.

"I want one of those soaps . . . not that one!" one woman says, pointing. When she gets what she's looking for, several others ask for the same thing. They are out of luck—it was, for today, one of a kind.

The sweet-smelling drawer may be overflowing or empty. Today it is full of tiny vials of perfume, plastic jars of moisturizer, paper-wrapped soaps, small containers of matching brands of shampoo and conditioner, and little bottles of bright green mouthwash. It is a trip around the world to read the labels of the donated items, most of which volunteers have picked up from hotels during their travels: the Grand Canyon, Tokyo, Nairobi, Paris.

Sometimes the drawer contains combs, shoe horns, shower caps, sewing kits. For fairness, there is a limit of two items per person. The guests have to make a choice: shampoo and conditioner? moisturizer and soap? Tomorrow there may be better brands or more choices or no choices at all.

Most men have trouble working the counter, though sometimes they get stuck doing it if a woman comes up and asks for something and they are just a few feet away. "One of the men was here for the first time, standing at the counter when one of the women asked him for a tampon," says Beverly. "Here he was, turning bright red, so I had to go over and rescue him."

~

Cleanup is a big part of the lunch operation. As soon as the cooking is finished, the dishwashing begins. Members of the Firm do the dishes. More than a hundred plates are used, and an even greater number of coffee cups need to be washed. With load after load, the dishwasher runs for a solid hour. Pots and pans almost as big as the enormous sinks in the kitchen need to be scrubbed and then sterilized. Beverly likes bossing around other members of the Firm. She says, "You're on pots today! You're doing it too slow. You're doing it the wrong way."

The managerial aspect is one of Beverly's great pleasures at Rosie's. She likes the idea of helping people, but she also has a good time. "I would hate doing it at my own house. At home, everything goes right in the dishwasher, but here I don't mind scrubbing pots and pans, and I don't mind putting things away."

The other members of the Firm kid Beverly about being in charge. "Look what she's making me do now!" they say, but everyone seems to like being here, even when the dining room gets rowdy. Her co-workers say to her, "I really feel good now. I feel like I did something, that maybe I'll go to heaven now if I do this every Friday."

There are a couple of people at the Firm Beverly would like to get to volunteer, but so far she has been unsuccessful. She understands their hesitancy, but she would like them to do it once. "I know if they tried coming, they'd like it."

~

Dessert is served every day. Sometimes it is homemade brownies or chocolate chip cookies; other times it is cut-up sheet cakes from a bakery or grocery store. Occasionally it's obvious that dessert is a leftover from a would-be celebration, such as a cake with pink frosting letters that read, "Happy Birthday, Eileen." Today, dessert is fudge bars, passed out by two volunteers who circulate through the dining room with soggy brown cardboard boxes. By the time dessert is served, most of the dishes are done and George can relax. He ambles from the kitchen into the dining room.

"What do you want for lunch next week?" he asks the women at one table as he wipes his face with an edge of his apron and slowly lowers his big frame into one of the vinyl chairs at a round table. "How about a nice chicken cutlet?" he offers before they have a chance to say anything.

"Only if we can have mashed potatoes with it," someone answers.

"Chicken cutlets it is," he proclaims, slamming his hand down on the table. The next week he will be in the kitchen, standing over a huge pot on the floor, mashing the potatoes.

Jack's piano often provides a soothing background to the clatter of dishes and voices in the room. Jack listens to music on his earphones on his way in to Rosie's, to get inspired, he says, then sits down at the piano and plays by ear. He puts together his own medleys from whomever he has heard while driving in. The women sometimes sing along softly to themselves at the table. This Friday one guest hums along to "*Que Sera, Sera*" as she turns the pages of her Danielle Steel paperback.

The music also serves to pump up the guests, especially those sitting close to the piano. They are the more vocal ones in the room, the ones who typically keep things rolling, talking loudly and laughing a lot. They get into the spirit of the day, request songs, yell suggestions. They sing along to Cole Porter and to Gershwin.

Jack just sits and plays through whatever is going on. One song blends into the next. He swings into "New York, New York," which gets several women clapping. Singing turns into dancing when three women get up on their feet. Other women whistle and laugh. The kitchen crew stops washing dishes to watch. People are having a great time.

Beverly remembers that on her first day at Rosie's, Jack played "God Bless America." The women got up and started singing, and Beverly had to go in the back because she started to cry. "It hit me that here are these women at a homeless shelter, and they're singing 'God Bless America' with all the spirit in the world."

As the time nears one o'clock, Jack's grand finale is "When the Saints Go Marching In." This time everybody sings. Two dancers are swinging each other around; a third grabs George from where he's been sitting.

When the women leave, a few stop to say thank you to Beverly for the lunch. "When they come up and thank me, I want to thank them for letting me do this," she says. "From the minute they get up to the time they go to bed, they have a task in front of them that I wouldn't want. They're trying to make new lives, to undo what's been done. They're trying to get back some of the dignity they've lost."

4

OPEN HOUSE

A TOURIST'S VIEW OF BOSTON probably includes the brownstones of Back Bay—one room wide and five stories high with tall windows and cobblestone sidewalks. Dorchester, however, is not Back Bay. Working-class people live in Dorchester. They are proud of where they are; it is home. In many cases, they cannot imagine living anywhere else. In this, the heart—pronounced "hot"—of the city, pure Boston is spoken, not the speech of the Brahmins or the Kennedys, but rather that distinctive form of Bostonspeak that is the equivalent of London cockney.

Rosie's home for women living with HIV is in a Dorchester neighborhood that looks like dozens of other neighborhoods in Boston. Behind chain-link fences, there are neat two- and three-story houses with small yards. "Tinmen" have been here; it's obvious that at one time the aluminum siding business was booming. White is the color of choice for most of the houses and also, in this part of town, for the occupants in this historically predominantly Polish neighborhood.

Rosie's new home is a long, narrow, three-story house on the only double lot on the street. Freshly planted mums in dark burgundy and off-white cluster around the front and sides of the gray-green house with the ivory trim. On the other side, a large, neatly tended yard gives a parklike feel to the property. There is no identifying plaque, nor is one planned.

Down the street, neighbors stand on the lawn of another house. Signs with circles and lines drawn through them decorate the chain-link fence surrounding the house: "No Hospice" and "No Menino" (the name of the Boston mayor who supported the contested occupancy permit).

There were many times it looked as if this Rosie's house were not going to happen. Boston's residential code allows up to four unrelated persons to live in an apartment, and plans called for the house to be divided into three apartments, thus easily allowing the planned ten women to live there. A building permit for construction was delayed for months, however, while the commissioner of the inspectional services department held additional neighborhood meetings to determine whether the house should be called residential or institutional. If it were determined to be the latter, it would fall under the jurisdiction of a dormant, no-member board that had been created a decade earlier to curb possible institutional expansion in Boston. James Kelly, president of the Boston City Council, argued a third viewpoint, that the house should be labeled a lodging house. As a lodging house, it would need a license from the city and a variance from the zoning board of appeals. Controversy swirled on all sides of the question. Ultimately, a review by the mayor's office determined that a simple occupancy permit was all that was needed, and the permit was granted.

Today, in an atmosphere reminiscent of a wedding or a festive birthday celebration, a large yellow-and-white striped tent stands in the yard by the house. The small tables underneath are loaded: some with shrimp, brownies, cookies, and macaroons, and others with big pots of coffee. Cold drinks are set out, but no alcohol.

It is a perfect sweater-weather fall day. The leaves are just starting to change on the few scattered trees along the block. The sky is blue and the air sparkles. Of the three porches off the back of the house, the top porch affords a view—if you look in just the right spot—of Boston Harbor as a tiny patch of blue squeezed between the houses. On this day, the water is sapphire, a couple of shades darker than the sky.

Everywhere people are walking through the house, talking with each other, introducing themselves—old friends, new friends. A small woman with braids approaches Molly Griffin, the manager of the new house. Molly gives her a long, silent, tearful hug. This woman will be moving into the house.

There is a lot of pride shown in the house. Many people have worked toward this day. A lot of the funding for the $1 million-plus capital project (which started off with a $10,000 donation from Pulitzer Prize–winning author Alice Walker) is still to be raised, but much of the work—the strategizing, the planning, the physical labor—has been done. A furniture store has provided at low cost ten rooms of bedroom furniture; interior designers have donated time and accessories; a church youth group has worked on the house.

Inside is the faint, clean smell of new construction mixed with polyurethane and paint. A long hallway, pale oak and blindingly glossy, runs down the middle of each of the three floors. Deep baseboards in each room are in contrast to the lack of moldings at the ceilings. Wall colors run to pale creams, slate blues, and roses; hardware gleams on the doors and windows.

On the first floor, the big dining room with its bay window is roomy enough for everyone in the house to gather for meals. Each of the three floors has a study. Each of the ten bedrooms has a small, tufted "lady's" chair and a twin bed with a brass headboard. Those are the only similarities among the bedrooms, however, because each is decorated with an attention to detail for just that room. The comforter in one has trailing ivy on a crisp white background; in another, the bed linens have an impressionist print in cranberry and green; the third is a colorful log cabin design. Small rugs add warmth to the hardwood floors. Matching towels are provided, and there are brand-new books on the nightstands. The window treatments vary—some are balloon shades and others are Priscilla curtains.

The bathrooms are roomy. Only the wide doorways and bars on the tubs hint at the hospital aspect of the house, as does the elevator that connects the three floors. Without these extra touches, the house would appear to be a typical renovated apartment building in any neighborhood.

Throughout the afternoon, people wind in and out of the rooms. On the stairways, people travel single-file up and down. A jazz singer named Rebecca Parris is among the visitors. Rebecca has been a friend of Kip Tiernan's for years and a friend to Rosie's as well. Rebecca is quiet today, keeping to herself. She is tall, with long, streaked hair, and wears a black slip dress. She goes upstairs and leans over the third-floor porch railing, taking a look at the neighborhood. Out the open windows wafts the sound of people talking and laughing. Over that runs the strong beat of scratchy recorded rap music from a house across the street.

"This is the one I like!" A small blonde girl gets through one bounce on a magenta-and-royal-blue bedspread before her mother sweeps her up and plants her back on the floor.

"Let's look at the other ones. What color do you think the one next door is?" her mother asks her, with a slightly embarrassed smile to a couple peering in the doorway.

A young woman walks through the third floor telling people that the program is going to start, and slowly the house begins to empty. People spill out the front and driveway doors onto the lawn.

After heartfelt welcomes from Kip and Executive Director Julie Brandlen, Rebecca Parris gets up to sing. Her voice is smoky as she calls out, "Hallelujah!" In the pause before she starts singing, rap music from across the street blares into the silence, accompanied by a bang, bang, bang.

Rebecca continues singing, "There's a place for us, somewhere a place for us. . . ." She sings *a cappella*—a strong, melodious rendition. On the grass Kip stands with her eyes closed, her hands clasped.

From a third-floor window across the street, the banging gets more insistent. Heads turn to locate the noise, the harsh sound of metal on metal. It is clearly no coincidence. It is making a statement.

"Hold my hand and we're halfway there, hold my hand and I'll take you there." Bang, bang, bang.

There is murmuring among the guests, some nervous giggling, exchanges of alarmed looks. A tension sweeps through the group.

Rebecca presses on, finishing the song. The banging stops. Several people are watching the house across the street to see if more will happen, but it is quiet. The music has been turned down or is being drowned out by the pickup of conversation among the people at the open house.

Someone asks Kip what she thinks about this. Should they worry? "We're going to just love them to death," Kip says, clear of her stand in all of this. "I consider this a flea on the navel of the universe."

As the party breaks up, neighbors stand on their front lawns. Visitors from the open house must walk by the "No Hospice" banners. Some exchange greetings with the neighbors, but most walk on. One person from the open house stops to talk to a neighbor about the Rosie's Place women moving in.

"Well, we're not happy. To have a hospital—with ambulances coming and going—foisted on us in a residential neighborhood, we're not happy at all. It doesn't belong here," the neighbor says angrily. "That doesn't mean we do not have compassion for the women, because we do."

The commitment to HIV-positive women began in 1991, when a three-bedroom apartment in one of Rosie's two auxiliary residences was rehabbed as a handicapped-accessible apartment for HIV-positive women. Molly Griffin, who had worked in social service programs for fifteen years and at the Hospice at Mission Hill, was hired to be the residence manager. Molly knew from her time spent working in the hospice that women usually have no one to care for them when they get sick, even though they have spent their lives taking care of their families.

As an increasing number of Rosie's guests went public with their HIV status, the board of directors of Rosie's Place decided to provide housing specifically for them. Subcommittees looked into it, and Julie Brandlen visited programs in Boston and New York.

There was agreement that the housing shouldn't be a halfway house or have an institutional setting. Everyone involved knew the project had to operate in line with the mission of Rosie's Place, but initially no one really knew exactly how that would be.

"I had a great opportunity to shape and create the program in 1991. We started small, with just three women, and wanted to find out what worked and what didn't," Molly says. "The whole process of getting into the house was so painful and prolonged at times, because of all the political shenanigans. Moving in there was really difficult."

For Molly, the house in Dorchester was a bit of a letdown. The women were really excited about moving to an aesthetically beautiful house, about being on a side street and having green space, but they didn't realize what would come along with the house. The population would more than triple in size, the staff would increase, and the coziness of the one, three-person apartment would be gone.

"When we couldn't be in each other's face all the time, everyone really missed that intimacy," Molly remarks.

It was decided to move slowly. The staff didn't start to interview women with HIV until the house had been open a couple of months. This gave the three women moving over from the apartment a chance to get acclimated. In the meantime, the people who work in the Boston AIDS community got the word out about the house.

With a growing number of women diagnosed with the virus as well as with full-blown AIDS, there was a large pool of candidates when the time came for interviews. The interviews were an ongoing process. "There's information we need to get," says Molly, "but it's really informal. We want women to know from the beginning that we're not an institution, we're not a program." Women staying at Rosie's in the overnight program were given priority because they were already part of the Rosie's family. Some were interested but understandably hesitant, Molly remembers. "They said, 'Oh, yeah, let me get back to you.'"

It was important to Rosie's to move the women in one by one, to consider the composition as the house filled up. As it happened, however, the second floor filled up all at once. By the end of the first year, the house was up to eight women, so there were two places to fill.

Moving in, Molly notes, is a big step. "The women have to break through a whole piece of denial. There are all these people, the staff, the visiting nurses. There's a honeymoon period of about two weeks where the women are so excited to have housing, to have support, and then they crash. They think, 'Oh my God, everybody here has the virus. How do I get close to somebody when I know eventually she's going to die? How do I take that risk?' "

The women can be anywhere along the HIV continuum. Some of them are asymptomatic and have jobs; others are seriously ill with opportunistic infections, the complications of AIDS. Visiting nurses and the same two nurse practitioners consistently come to the house. Molly sings their praises: "They are used to working in a poor community. They have been extraordinary with the staff and the women. It's crucial to making things work."

"A lot of things I can do myself," adds Molly, for whom there is no such thing as a typical day. Solid, capable, and reassuring, Molly, with her friendly green eyes, exudes an air of being able to cope with anything. Her warmth draws the women in, and her capability helps make them feel taken care of. She has completed a nursing degree since coming to Rosie's.

Most of the women living in the house have had problems with addiction, according to Molly. "I haven't met a woman yet who doesn't have a history of serious trauma of some kind." There is no requirement that a woman have a specific amount of drug-free time to move into the house. She has only to promise that she's willing to work on it, and her promise is taken in good faith. "To keep that open-door policy," Molly continues, "you always have to give another chance and to be true to the mission. Women are treated in a dignified, respectful manner, as adults, and you don't infantilize or institutionalize the women."

To work with women who are so fragile, who are in crisis day in and day out, is hard work. Four staff people and two college students live with the women. The college students receive credit for living and working there. Dinner is prepared every night, and the women may opt for that or arrange for their own meals. Refrigerators are stocked in each apartment according to a shopping list compiled by the women. Bulk items come through the dining room at Rosie's Place; otherwise, shopping is done at a grocery store. "We try to accommodate what the women need," Molly says.

Some of the women spend a lot of time visiting between apartments. A few who work are gone for most of the day. Activities are planned for any who are interested. Some women are, of course, more ill than others. There are always staff people and volunteers to help out. The women's individual bedrooms allow for privacy when they want or need it; when they choose to be together, they can gather in the living room and dining room.

The Rosie's Place network reaches the house not only in the form of food and maintenance but also in the form of tickets to special events. One week the women may go to an ice show or to see a play in the theater district, such as the long-running *Shear Madness,* or they may go out to dinner. Sometimes they go farther afield. Molly's sister has opened her house on Cape Cod to the women for a weekend now and then. "There is no agenda there, we just go and hang out, and the women can do whatever they want. It's great."

There are, of course, celebrations for the holidays, for birthdays, for sobriety dates. Holidays are a stressful time for all homeless women, who have memories of and wishes for better times. For the women at the house, holidays also bring the inevitable thought: "Will this be my last Thanksgiving? My last Christmas?" For one woman in the house, last Christmas was the first Christmas she had celebrated since she was eleven years old. At age twelve, she had hit the streets. She had never even had a birthday party, so at age thirty-nine she had her first birthday party at the house in Dorchester.

The first holiday celebrated at the house was Thanksgiving. "All the women said they hated holidays, don't bother to get a turkey," Molly says. "Well, we all ate together—a big dinner in the main dining room for the six women living there at the time, plus staff. We had a turkey. I burned the butter, and the fire alarm went off. It was the funniest thing."

Controversy over Christmas quickly followed, according to Molly. "The women began to object to

Top: *A group of staffers and guests with Kip Tiernan (far left in front) and Julie Brandlen (next to Kip).*
Middle: *Rosie's Place main building at 889 Harrison Avenue in Boston's South End.*
Bottom: *Current guest in main lobby, in front of portrait of Natasha, the very first guest of Rosie's Place.*

Top Left: *Liza Minnelli, host of a special benefit at Boston's Harborlights Pavilion to support A Positive Step. Other celebrity supporters shown here are enjoying themselves at "Lunch with Lily and the Ladies."* **Top Right:** *Rosie O'Donnell with Kip Tiernan.* **Above:** *(left to right) Kathleen Doxer, Teresa Heinz, Julie Brandlen.* **Right:** *(top to bottom) Local newscasters Lila Orbach, Susan Wornick, Natalie Christian, Hank Phillippi Ryan.* **Far Right:** *Lily Tomlin as Madame Lupe.*

Top: *The Rosie's Place house for women living with HIV.* **Middle:** *Living room on first floor.* **Bottom:** *The first residence manager.*

Top: *Guest/volunteer in the clothing room.* **Middle Left and Right:** *Staffer (left) and Rosie's guest with Patriots Cheerleader Julie LaMarca (right) on board the Odyssey Cruise around Boston Harbor.* **Bottom:** *A guest upstairs at Rosie's.*

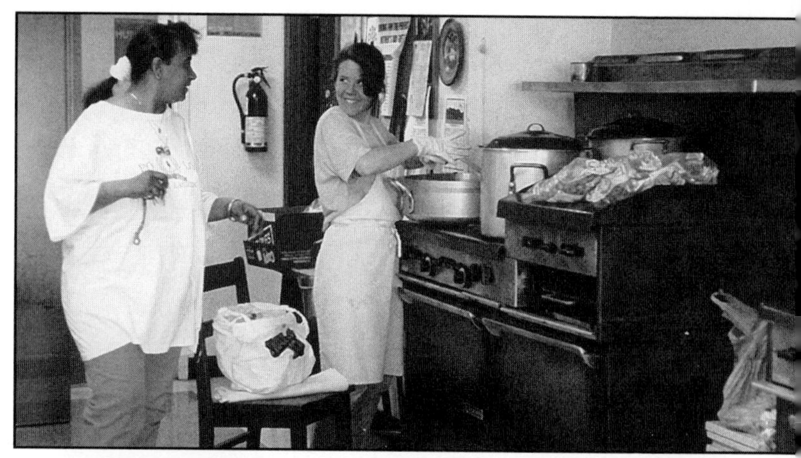

Typical scenes from Friday lunch at Rosie's Place. **Top Left:** *Guest/volunteer chats a moment with staffer who often drives the van.* **Above:** *George Keady and Aggie Cahill fill plates.* **Right:** *Beverly Strasnick dishes out fruit.* **Far Right Top:** *Staffer greets two guests.* **Far Right Middle:** *Guest gets a beverage.* **Far Right Bottom:** *Guest enjoys the soup (left), and volunteer helps with clean-up (right).*

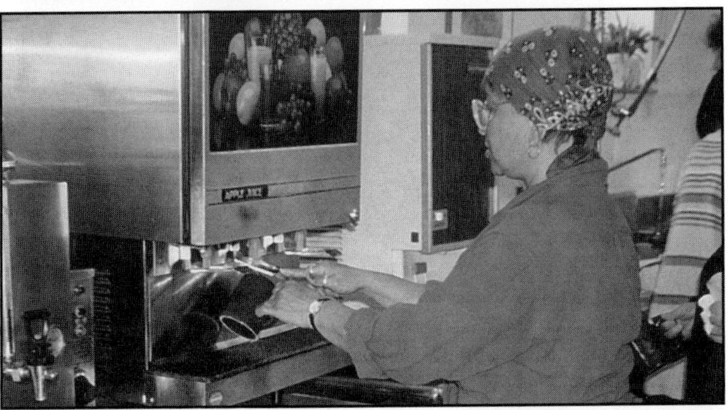

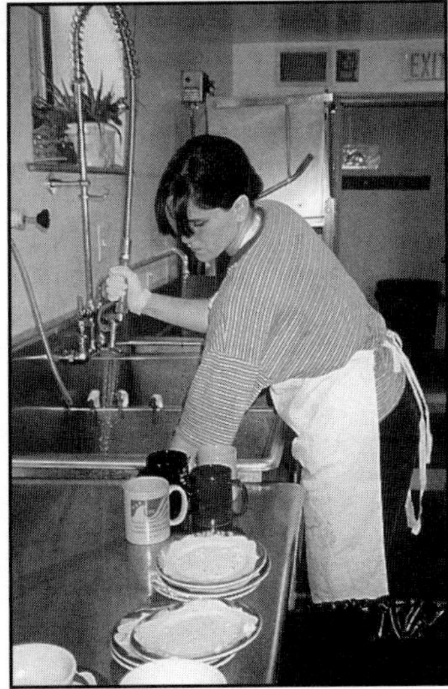

Social events at Rosie's may raise needed funds or may be just for fun. **Top:** *Guests and staffers take turns modeling at the fashion show on the terrace at Rosie's, just for fun.* **Middle:** *Dancing guests join staff members at a Share Your Heart fund-raising party in February.* **Bottom:** *Kip Tiernan and Boston Mayor Thomas Menino at the Share Your Heart party.*

that one. They said no way did they want to do anything for Christmas—they hated that holiday, they didn't want a tree." Even so, a big tree went up on the first floor in front of the bay windows, followed by smaller trees on the second and third floors. The women who had objected the most, the ones who had been most vocal about hating the holidays, were the ones who ended up decorating the most, Molly notes. "We went out and got all kinds of gifts, picture frames, clothing, CDs, and one really special gift for each woman. If a woman had children, we made sure there were gifts for her kids at the house. We still do that."

For one woman, that first Christmas at the house was the first time in twenty years she had been drug free. "Of course there are lots of ups and downs," Molly notes. "We know that's going to happen, but the holidays are really great times, incredible times at the house."

Some of the nicest times at the house are not the special occasions but the informal times spent hanging out together. "Somebody always puts coffee on and we talk about what's going on," says Molly. "Unlike their dealings with the welfare system and the health care system, we allow the women to give. The women have a lot of love to give, a lot of talent. You can't not let them do that.

"Even if you have a network, and people are supporting you, it's still really hard [to stay drug free].

When you're homeless and either there's no one there or they don't believe you because they've heard it so many times before, you feel like a failure all the time. It seems unreasonable to me to say, 'Come back in three months.' So we work with the women from the beginning, realizing that relapse is always a part of the process. We're realistic. We say, 'Okay, it happens. Let's go on. Isn't it incredible that you can keep on trying?'

"We are asking women to give up the only thing that has consistently eased their pain. There is that half hour of relief before the remorse sets in," Molly says. It is an important part of Rosie's mission to be there to offer help when the women try again.

Frannie was one of the three women who came to the house in Dorchester from Rosie's original HIV apartment. By that time, her AIDS was well advanced. Frannie was a quiet woman, a gentle person who kept to herself, and she was addicted to crack cocaine. She had an associate of arts degree in early childhood education—she was good with children and liked them. She also had a son who had already lost his father to AIDS.

"Frannie had the most incredible fourteen-year-old son. He was motivated in school, interested in sports. She adored him," Molly recalls. "She wanted to be there when he graduated from high school. That was her goal."

Frannie was a nonjudgmental person. She understood that in order not to be judged herself, she could not judge other people. Generally, she didn't share much and didn't complain, but three or four times she broke down with Molly. One time when they were sitting together, talking about how Frannie could keep from going out and getting high again, she put her head in Molly's lap and sobbed, "I don't want to die, I'm too young to die. Do you think I deserve this? Are you going to remember me?"

"Her life was so painful," observes Molly. "She lit up when she talked about her son, but she felt tremendously guilty that she was robbing him of his mother. Frannie said, 'Am I going to see him graduate, am I? Tell me I am.' And I told her no, I don't think you are. She was so intense I was just reeling with it."

At one point, Frannie relapsed and disappeared for a short time from the Rosie's community. "I got the word out on the street that I was looking for her," says Molly. "I thought if she had enough trust to call back, I would know we were doing something right. When I talked to her, she was ashamed that she had let me down." Frannie returned.

From that point on, whenever Frannie got sick she would call Molly from the hospital and ask her to bring her what she needed. Molly always went, but she also sent each new staff member to visit so that Frannie could make a connection with someone other than Molly.

Sometimes when Frannie got out of the hospital she would drift back to the streets. "Unfortunately," Molly says, "I think Frannie gave up early on. I think she was beaten down by the virus much earlier than the virus actually caught up with her and came back."

Talking with Molly, Frannie would cry, "I'm thirty-six and I'm going to die. My son is going to be alone—he won't even remember me. My life is a waste. My family doesn't want anything to do with me."

Molly doesn't know how close Frannie was to any of her family. "I've learned to try not to judge how families operate. My priority is for the women."

As time went on, Frannie became sicker and sicker. At one point, after another stay in the hospital, she came home weighing about eighty pounds, barely able to walk. "She went out and got high one last time," Molly remembers. "It amazed me, but that's how terrified she was."

Frannie's relapses were becoming disruptive to the whole house. "But the women in the house feel that everyone deserves to keep on getting chances because they realize this could be any of them," Molly says. "Somehow *they* found what it took to get clean, and Frannie hadn't been able to tap that yet. She was starting to open up. They wanted to give her that chance."

Finally, Frannie made a deal with Molly that she would go into a drug treatment program. A few months later, Frannie stabilized and celebrated her thirty-seventh birthday in the house. All she wanted was a birthday party in her own house, where her own family could come, so that's what the women of the house gave her. She had never had family in her own home before. Her mother came, along with her two grandmothers, her aunts, her son, and the staff members of the house.

"What women's biological families don't understand is that we [in the house] become a kind of family—we're there day to day. Oftentimes we can be unconditional, because we're in a place where we *can* be," Molly points out. Frannie's birthday party gave her a chance to reconnect with her family, and the house provided a safe place for them to come and visit her.

Over the next few months, Frannie continued to slip away with a condition that caused her brain to deteriorate. There was no treatment, no prophylactic or symptomatic management. She went back and forth to Boston City Hospital. She eventually lost the ability to speak, though she could still understand people. Her son spent a lot of time at the house. "It must have been excruciating," Molly says. "Frannie hadn't told me definitely she wanted to stop the course of treatment, but she had indicated that. We took her to the emergency room, and she was able to let them know she wanted to stop everything except pain management.

"Frannie was one of the first women who came to Rosie's with HIV and the first one to die at the house. I was in the room with her when she died, sharing the most intimate piece of a person's life. It was as if Frannie needed permission to let go, and the message the women in the house sent to her was: You can leave—we're really going to miss you, but we'll be okay. So we came full circle; she gave me the incredible gift of closure."

The night that Frannie died, three of the women in the house never went to bed. She died surrounded by these women in the house where she wanted to be. With the pain controlled by morphine, she was comfortable, and her seizures were kept under control. As the women talk about Frannie now, there is a lot of laughing along with the crying.

"We [staff] were being watched," Molly observes. "Were we being respectful? Loving? Were we being supportive, allowing Frannie to die with dignity? There was a huge sense of relief among the women that her death was handled the way she wanted it. That's the comforting part. But the women were also watching their sister die with the very thing that would kill them."

There was a family funeral service. For Molly, the most heartbreaking part of the funeral was the presence of Frannie's son. "He asked Frannie's housemates if they were going to be okay."

The women at the house followed the funeral with a memorial service of their own, which they held on the third-floor porch. They talked about Frannie, did readings, and released helium balloons that contained their own messages that might be discovered much later or far away. "This is an incredible family," Molly says. "The women are an inspiration and they don't even know it."

~

Frannie's room on the first floor was kept empty for a while to honor her. Eventually another woman moved in and became a member of the family. Molly remarks that the house in Dorchester has turned out to be an excellent choice. Once the women were all moved in, there were no more problems with the neighbors. One abutter moved away. As for the person who had been banging through "There's a Place for Us," the house members have never seen him or her.

Sometimes neighbors stop Molly on the street to ask how things are going. A couple of them have said, "Boy, it's really quiet over there!" Whatever they anticipated or whatever they feared from HIV-positive women or from poor women or maybe even from black women does not seem to be a problem.

"I feel like Rosie's Place has helped to educate people in this neighborhood," concludes Molly. "We've really helped break that stereotype. The women are invested in their home, and they want it to look good. In the first year, we had ambulances maybe four times. These are great women, not crazy women, not out-of-control women.

"It's a common misconception that to work with people who are terminally ill, or women who have AIDS or have experienced trauma—that it's a depressing thing. It's not true. If you walked into that house, you would not think it was an AIDS house or a house full of death. Somebody is always in pain, but someone is always laughing."

Since Frannie died, Molly says things are up and down. "There's a whole lot of anger. What's really good is that the women are pretty clear about what the anger is about."

5

OVERNIGHT

Dinner at Rosie's Place is served seven nights a week. Volunteers arrive at 4:00 p.m. to help get the meal ready by 6:00. The doors open to Rosie's guests at 4:30. It is during dinnertime that many women make decisions about where they will spend the night. Armed with clipboards, staffers make their way around the dining room, checking to see who needs a place to stay. They move between the dining room and the office, making phone calls to find out what beds are available and where.

At 8:00 the dining room closes. The women who are staying overnight at Rosie's—a maximum of twenty at one time—go upstairs or outside until the 9:00 overnight-program curfew time. Most of the rest of Rosie's guests go down the street on foot or to the corner to catch a bus. A few wait by the door. In early fall in Boston, it is dark by 7:00. The shoe factory across the street is barely lit, contributing to the late-night feel of the neighborhood. As they burst out of Rosie's, the women create an explosion of noise and life in the darkness.

Those by the front door talk and laugh together as they wait to get into a battered blue van—the shelter shuttle—for the nightly ride to a shelter. With a staff person or a volunteer at the wheel, the shuttle will wind through the streets, its route varying according to where the women need to go—the places that have been found for them to spend the night.

This is a warm, even balmy night for late September. It's Friday, and the mood is jovial as the women kid around with the driver. After a handful of women impulsively decide to walk rather than ride, the driver, a staff member this time, climbs into the fifteen-passenger van. Sometimes the van needs to go out twice, full on both trips, but tonight's load is light, just eight passengers, including a volunteer for company. The women climb into the back three rows of seats.

"Can I sit in front tonight?" one asks as she's about to climb in.

"Sorry, no, that seat's taken," the driver tells her. The coveted seat next to the driver, the "shotgun" position, had been spoken for before everyone even got outside. Several other women request it as they enter the van, but when they are told it's taken there is no argument.

"Will you drive me to Charlestown?" one of the passengers asks, naming a town several miles beyond the usual delivery-stop radius.

"Sure, no problem!" the driver tells her, laughing.

The first stop is Boston City Hospital, only a block from Rosie's. The driver edges into a narrow driveway to get to the back of the building, barely able to turn the stubborn steering wheel in the direction she wants. The women who get off here either will stay at the hospital's shelter, called In-Take, or will take another bus to a shelter called Long Island. Each night, ten busloads of men and women travel to Long Island. Most of the runs are between 7:00 and 8:00, with a couple of buses leaving at 10:00. As a practical matter, no pregnant women or obviously sick people go to the Long Island shelter.

As the van from Rosie's comes around to the back of the hospital, it just misses the curb of the narrow, curving driveway. A police car's open door is the next invitation to a fender-bender, practically inviting the cumbersome van to shear it off. The driver avoids it. Straight ahead is the bus stop, but before transferring to the bus for Long Island or entering In-Take, the men and women seeking shelter must stand in single file, each with a bag or two, in a chain-link chute. A single powerful beam lights up the faces and fronts of those in line, leaving the surroundings in darkness. A man with a clipboard checks each person in, one at a time, directing them through the door and down the hall, until at last they're out of sight.

Two women from Rosie's jump out with their bags, call good-bye to those left on board, and take their place at the back of the line in the chain-link chute. As the van moves down the street, someone emerges from the subway stop in the almost-deserted intersection near the hospital. A woman on the van says the stop is "the most notorious corner in Boston." Why is that? she is asked. "Prostitution," she answers, quickly supplying the explanation.

The driver tugs at the reluctant steering wheel and continues on. All the destinations this evening are within a few blocks of Rosie's. The mood remains jovial; it may be the unseasonably warm weather or the spaciousness of the less-than-full van. It is easy to imagine these women are on their way to a party, not to shelters.

Three women on the way to their subway stop get off sooner than they have to. Tonight they want to take advantage of the warm, breezy air and prefer to walk a few extra blocks. Another of the passengers says she wants to go home with the driver, so there's no need to bother dropping her off anywhere.

"People always want to go home with me," the driver responds. Everyone laughs. Someone else asks the driver her age, and she supplies it by stating the year she was born. At age twenty-five she is clearly at least a decade or two younger than her passengers.

The next stop is a few blocks away, down a quiet side street at another shelter, where a uniformed man checks women in at the door. The last two women get out, pause briefly to speak with the guard, and go up a few steps to the inner door of the building.

The van usually goes also to the huge Pine Street Inn, probably the best known of Boston's shelters and one that takes both men and women. Its other stop would be Dudley Station, a central location to get buses to Roxbury and Dorchester. Since neither is a stop on tonight's route, the van run is over in twenty-five minutes.

"People were in a great mood tonight. A lot of it is not being crowded," the driver explains to the volunteer. "When everybody's bundled and crowded and can't get out, it puts everyone in the worst mood."

Back at Rosie's, there are still two people cleaning up in the kitchen. The driver greets them, then does her last task of the day, securing the building for the alarm system. She makes her rounds, checking all the windows and doors to make sure they are locked.

Rosie's overnight program houses women for ten days, thirty days, or an extended stay. The ten-day stay is called the emergency program. Upstairs, the staff person for the night checks in a new, emergency-program guest, who has ended up at Rosie's from South America via Canada. She is small, with long dark hair and light skin. She is neatly dressed in a skirt and blouse, dark stockings, dressy flat shoes, and a coat.

She explains that she is hoping to find a job within the next two weeks. The staff member tells her she can stay for ten days, and she can be there with no questions asked as long as she abides by the following rules:

- Each woman is allowed to bring three medium-sized boxes or bags of belongings and ten hanging items.

- There is a 9:00 P.M. curfew, with lights out in the rooms at 11:30.
- No visitors are allowed in the rooms.
- The women must be out of bed by 7:00 A.M. except on weekends.
- There is no television during the day.
- Snacking is not permitted during the day, but coffee, tea, and juice are provided.
- No laundry can be started after 10:00 P.M.
- No one can cook after 11:00 P.M.

The more important rules are: No alcohol or illegal drug use in the building; no one enters the building under the influence of alcohol or drugs; and there can be no weapons, abusive behavior, or acts of violence toward anyone.

"Okay," the new guest says, a smile never leaving her face as she listens to the rules. She is painfully polite. "Okay," she says again, softly.

She asks whether she can use the telephone, and she is told that she can, but only for business calls. She asks how she can get in touch with friends, and she is told that she can use the pay phone in the hall. She is only allowed to use it for ten minutes at a time, however.

She needs money for carfare, which the staffer assures her will be provided. Carfare, meals, and a bed are part of the emergency program, as is daily contact with a staff advocate just to touch base. She is told where she can keep her valuables, at which point she explains she has no valuables. The staffer hands her a towel and a bar of soap, and she climbs the stairs to her room.

As each woman comes in for the night, the staff member or volunteer goes down to the front door to let her in. No evening guests are allowed. Because everyone who is staying overnight must be in by 9:00 P.M., the front door buzzer seems to ring constantly between 8:00 and 9:00. Each time it rings, either the staffer or the one volunteer on duty peers through the window of the door and then lets a woman in after making sure her name is on the checklist for the night. Once inside, the woman either will go straight upstairs to her assigned room or will stop in the living room to see who's around.

Tonight one of the women makes the deadline by seconds but then immediately ducks back out to throw up in the bushes outside the door. How sick is she? The staff person on duty comes down to see if she wants to go to the hospital, which is a block away.

"No, I don't want to sit in the emergency room all night," she softly sighs. "I'll just go up to bed. If I don't feel better in the morning, then I'll go."

The volunteer helps the sick woman carry her things up the first few stairs and then across to the other side of the building where the elevator will take them the rest of the way. By the time they reach the top floor, the volunteer must prop the woman up as they make their way down the hall and into the room. A woman sitting on one of the other beds in the room jumps up, clearly agitated, when the two of them come in.

"What are you doing here?" she demands of the volunteer. Then her gaze switches to the sick woman. "You're not allowed to entertain in your room!" she exclaims. The volunteer, who had no idea she was violating a rule against staff-only in bedrooms, is taken aback.

Falling into her bed, the sick woman whips her head around to look at the volunteer. "You're not staff? I thought you were!" The volunteer quickly steps into the hall, absorbing the sick woman's message and stunned by the fury of the room's other occupant.

(The volunteer has privileges the paid staff member does not, however. Once all the women have gone to bed, the volunteer can stretch out on one of the couches and go to sleep. The staffer, on the other hand—as the person responsible for the safety of the women—has to stay up all night.)

Friday is the night of the weekly house meeting, which is run by the staff member on duty. There are rules to go over, as well as a review of the policies of living at Rosie's Place, including cleaning up after yourself and being considerate.

The meeting takes place in the cream-colored living/dining area, a space about 11 feet by 34 feet. It is adjacent to a small kitchen that only the twenty overnight guests may use. Women sit in molded plastic chairs around the room's three tables or settle into the vinyl cushions of the room's two wood-sided couches. Everything is tidy. Magazines are stacked neatly in compartments at the base of the coffee table. Miniblinds hang neatly in the windows; healthy plants rest on each sill. A large television set sits in the middle of the room, its screen blank during the meeting.

There is exactly enough seating for the twenty women staying there. The staff member stands while leading the meeting.

"There is a reason every woman is here," she tells Rosie's guests. "Something has happened to her in her life; you should be aware of that and be good to each other." The overnight program makes Rosie's Place a home for women, a sanctuary from their treatment outside. It is a safe place where women are treated with respect. In return they are expected to be kind to each other and not diminish each other's dignity.

Sometimes the women have a talking circle during which a "talking stick" is passed around. Whoever possesses the stick may talk, but it is not needed tonight. The issues are universal but not earthshaking. They are the inevitable petty annoyances that occur in communal living. Problems with sharing a refrigerator dominate the meeting tonight. "I bought an ice cream sundae," one woman says. "I was looking forward to that sundae all week, and when I went to get it, it was gone."

Silence.

"I wouldn't mind if someone bought another one and gave me a bite, but I was looking forward to that sundae."

More silence. She looks around the room, not accusingly but as if asking for support. She makes eye contact with a few women; the rest are staring at the floor or in another direction.

The staff member steps in with a reminder, "Stealing someone's food is stealing, and stealing is a reason to make you lose your bed." Then, shifting to a related concern, she continues, "Please don't buy two weeks' worth of groceries and put them in there because there won't be room for everything. And make sure everything is labeled."

The esthetics of the refrigerator bother one young guest, who complains that people are leaving food in it for too long. "I know for a fact that three-quarters of a sub sandwich has been in there for two weeks," she says. "Some of that stuff is disgusting. People should take their food outta there."

The staff member agrees, pointing out that nothing should be kept for more than a week. "One person's in charge of the refrigerator, of washing it down and cleaning out the old food," she reminds the women. "Whose job was it to do it this past week?" The young woman who complained about the refrigerator raises her hand. "Well, that was me." Everyone laughs. She does, too. The woman next to her slaps her on the back.

Before the meeting is adjourned, jobs for the coming week are handed out—morning and evening chores. They range from cleaning the kitchen and scouring a bathroom, chores no one likes, to the one job everyone likes, watering the plants. There are no complaints, though, because it is a rotating job list. When the meeting breaks up, mops and sponges are handed out for the week.

Some women go to bed after the meeting, but others stick around. Everyone may stay up late Friday night because there is no mandatory wake-up time on weekends. The kitchen is stocked with food since Rosie's doesn't serve lunch on Saturdays. Salad greens and hamburger patties are in the refrigerator. Bananas and pineapples sit on the counter, along with large bins of wheat bread, raisin bread, and English muffins. A full juice dispenser is also on the counter, and coffee and tea are always available. A few women hurry from the meeting into the kitchen to make late-night sandwiches for themselves or to toast raisin bread before the 11:00 cooking deadline.

One woman takes two eggs from the refrigerator and places them in a bowl of water in the microwave oven. The results are explosive to say the least. Tempers erupt as egg shells fly. "I'm sorry, I didn't know," she apologizes. She has to repeat her apology a couple of times before a fellow occupant of the kitchen, truly shaken up by what happened, stops sputtering.

A woman in a nightgown and fuzzy slippers stretches out on the couch until the staff member reminds her it's against the rules to take all three cushions. Her sigh is more visible than audible as she sits up and puts her feet firmly on the floor. Simple math explains the seemingly arbitrary rule: There are six spaces on the sofas for the twenty women staying overnight.

The staff member produces the entertainment of the night: a videotape with a choice of three movies that have been taped from a movie channel. The tape is put into the VCR and several women settle down to watch. The women need to agree: It's this or television. A nightshirted guest wanders down from upstairs, where she has been giving herself a facial. She sits down in one of the molded chairs, her face covered with a ghostly white mask that glows faintly in the darkened room. They decide to watch the first movie, which is family-type entertainment. The second and third selections are action films with plenty of gunfire, and they are vetoed by the group as "guy movies."

The woman with the facial mask wants to see if "Soul Train" is on the television. There is no newspaper around, no listing from the Sunday paper or a *TV Guide,* so she keeps switching from the movie to the television to see if she can find it. The other women are patient, for the most part keeping quiet while she frantically switches channels.

This is a quiet Friday night. By 1:00 A.M., everyone is out of the living room, and the volunteer who is staying overnight can get some sleep.

The staff member, up for the night, spends her time making rounds and doing paperwork in the staff office at the top of the stairs from the main floor. During the day, three staff members occupy the office, but at night, there is only one staffer. Down the hall from the office is a stark white bathroom with a double sink, two toilet stalls, and two showers. Beyond that is a laundry room with two washers, two dryers, and an ironing board that is kept set up. Sometimes, as the night wears on, the overnight staffer's biggest challenge is staying awake. More often, one of the guests comes in to talk. There, in the quiet, is a way to make contact.

In the morning, the women slowly drift into the living/dining area, which is lit by sunshine. Since it is Saturday morning, the pace is leisurely. Someone starts coffee. Others make toast and cereal for themselves. A couple of women fry hamburgers from the communal stash of food in the refrigerator. After they are done, the volunteer cooks breakfast for anyone who wants ham and eggs. One woman asks for her eggs over easy and another woman for sunny-side up. A third woman takes a chance on scrambled eggs and sits down to eat with the volunteer.

The two women talk casually. Each explains how she came to Boston from another part of the country.

Finding common ground, the women go on to talk about their children. The guest tells the volunteer how, many years ago when she was unable to find a good nursery school for her children, she started a cooperative venture with other parents. Now one of her children has a baby of her own. "I don't know how I'll ever do it, but I hope I can go to California sometime and see her," says the guest, slowly beginning to stand. As she starts back to her room, she tells the volunteer, "Thanks. I wasn't really hungry, but I enjoyed talking." Her plate is still full.

As breakfasts cook and the women talk, the staff member waits for her relief person to show up. Like many of the staff at Rosie's, she is going to school and needs to juggle working with studying, writing papers, and spending time with her kids. For some staff members, working with poor or homeless women has sparked an interest in getting an advanced human services degree.

Today, the woman assigned to early morning plant watering is enjoying her job for the week. "I like to do this, it makes me feel good." A little while later, she stops by the laundry room and helps the volunteer fold two dryer loads of dish towels from the dining room. The two women may not sit down together to talk, but the simple act of working together brings a sense of easy companionship.

~

No stranger to the overnight routines at Rosie's Place, Tiara Washington has known Rosie's both as a guest and as a staff member. She has had eight children, lost them all to foster care, and after a seven-year struggle, has gotten every one of them back. A grandmother at age forty, she lives with her younger children in a large rented house a few miles from Rosie's. Occasionally she comes back but just to visit. Tiara remembers when she first came to stay overnight at Rosie's.

"Oh, those were the good times!" she says. "That was the beginning of a new chapter in my life, the beginning of the end of my drug experience. There was a new sense of direction."

On her first night, though, she was actively using drugs. Still, she decided she wanted to try Rosie's month-long program. She felt it could give her the stability she needed. "I decided I wanted this thirty-day program. I wanted it so bad, but I had to be drug-free," she remembers. When staff advocates decide that a woman can benefit from more time in the program, they are allowed to give her one or more extensions. As she battled her addiction, Tiara spent a total of 151 days in the program.

"They were strict," Tiara remembers. "You had to be on time. You couldn't stay out all night. You had to be home at 9:00. What adult is going to be in at 9:00 at night in the summertime? We weren't allowed to even sit out on the front stoop with our friends, who we knew were out there. No lookin' out the window shit. We had to be up at 7:00—out of the bed, not just awake. You had to do your morning chore, and if you were cooking you had to be up at 6:00."

Getting up at 6:00 or 7:00, even if there are medical or housing appointments, leaves a long day to fill. In the beginning of her stay at Rosie's, Tiara spent time with her boyfriend. He, too, was in the homeless cycle. "He was staying in shelters, and that's how we met. At the beginning, we'd go to the park and have picnics. We were able to buy some food. I took chicken to the [Boston] Common, or I picked up bologna or peanut butter and jelly and made sandwiches. We'd go to the movies. He took me to places I hadn't been."

Tiara had grown up in Boston. She is the oldest of eight children, and she was the first of her siblings to have her own baby when she was a teenager. Then she had a second child, and though she still wanted to finish high school, she couldn't manage it with two babies. Eventually, she had six more children. When her youngest was two years old, there was a devastating electrical fire in Tiara's apartment. Everyone got out uninjured, but the Department of Social Services (DSS) took her children away temporarily.

After her children were returned to her, Tiara had to deal with eight kids, the pressure of trying to relocate, and substance addiction. All of these things led to risky behavior. Within a few months, DSS removed the children again, this time with the goal of adoption.

"Both drugs and alcohol have played a big part in my life," Tiara says, nodding. "DSS said I was neglecting my children, and they were right, but I couldn't stand to have my kids go away alone, without seeing a familiar face. They ended up going two by two, to foster homes." Her two youngest children were not returned to her until they were nine years old, although she saw them off and on during the seven-year period. Her other children were returned sooner, but it took several years.

While her children were in foster care, Tiara stayed in various shelters. Many nights she took the bus out to Long Island from Boston City Hospital. "I made sure my butt was on that bus," she says. Still, it wasn't easy, scrambling to find a place to sleep every night. It was in the course of her rounds of the shelters that she found Rosie's Place and stayed a week. Because of the way the overnight programs at Rosie's were set up then, the week's stay meant that she could not come back for two weeks. The thirty-day program was just beginning. When two of Tiara's friends applied, she also applied and was accepted.

When Tiara's thirty-day program was almost over, the director asked her if she wanted to make twenty dollars by mopping the dining room floor. Tiara washed the floor and was paid. Then the director asked if she wanted to help out in the main office—answering the phone, directing the calls, taking messages, and opening the door for people. She again agreed. Thanks to extensions, the job that was supposed to be for one day lasted for six months—while Tiara was still living at Rosie's and for a short time after she moved out.

The job felt great to Tiara. She not only got paid, she was also able to dress for an office. She selected her clothes from Rosie's clothing room. "For the first time in my life I went out to lunch, and that made me feel like a normal person," Tiara remembers.

She also remembers some of the more unsettling aspects of her new life. At night, living upstairs at Rosie's consisted of "waiting in line for the phone, girlfriend time, and going through donations before they hit the clothing room. I had been washing clothes, sharing food with a friend at night. When I started working downstairs it kind of broke my friend's heart because there was no more hanging out together. I was working in the main office, and she was trying to succeed in the thirty-day program. My friend thought I became uppity, but I didn't. I just became professional."

Though some of Tiara's fellow guests encouraged her to keep her desk job at Rosie's, the man she was seeing did not. He missed her company, and he worried about the changes he saw in her. "When I started working, my boyfriend felt like he was losing me. He knows that the women there preach to you about getting up on your own two feet. He thought I was turning my back on us, putting our relationship on the back burner just because I was at Rosie's, listening to the women there."

After Tiara left Rosie's, she got her own apartment. Her goal was to come back eventually to Rosie's as a staff member, but Rosie's has a six-month rule: Guests need to stay away for half a year before returning as staff members. The reasoning is that many of the people who have known the guest as a guest will have left in six months. Thus, after six months, guests who become staff members can function comfortably in their new positions, without former compatriots—consciously or unconsciously—trying to keep them in their old roles. Even so, when Tiara was hired six months later to work as an assistant dining room supervisor, a lot of people remembered her. It made no difference in her case, since she had *seemed* to be a staff member for so long.

Tiara still had a lot to learn as a new staff member. "I knew nothing at first. I had to plan meals, order food, cook. My first year there I had a great supervisor who pulled no punches. Her attitude was, 'You got this position, that means you can handle it. I'm not going to baby you. You're going to have to fight for it.'"

There are few staff positions at Rosie's Place, so the bulk of the workforce is made up of volunteers. Tiara had to learn to supervise an ever-changing work crew. She soon realized it wasn't a good idea to ask a volunteer to do anything she was not willing to do herself, such as taking out the trash, washing pots, and mopping floors. Rosie's made her, she feels, more alert, more considerate, and kinder than she used to be. "I'm a naturally good person but I had a nasty attitude. I found out I could not keep doing things the way I had been. It just wasn't working. You catch more flies with honey than vinegar. The vinegar wasn't working. People didn't want to be around me at first. So I started putting on the honey. I started having fun.

"All I wanted to do was help people. Social services was where I wanted to be, but I did not have the schooling for it. I never had the training. In the dining room at Rosie's I could help women the way I always wanted to. I could give them support and let them know I was there, that there was a light at the end of their tunnel. I've seen some people make it, but I've also seen them relapse and try again."

Sarah Rose is one of the people Tiara has known over the years at Rosie's, someone whom she admires and respects. "When I first started coming here, Sarah Rose was still getting high. I've watched her become a success. She's a wonderful person, the comedian of the bunch. When her table [in the dining room] has a conflict going on, she's the peacemaker."

During her time at Rosie's, Tiara saw a lot of women turn their lives around. The women knew that Tiara had been where they were now, and they felt that if she had made it, they could, too. Some started asking her if they could help clean up at night. They didn't want to leave when the dining room closed at 8:00. Helping to clean up was a way to stay, and they liked that.

After working at Rosie's for more than a year, Tiara was selected for a culinary arts program scholarship. Though she was glad to have an opportunity to build a career, she had misgivings about continuing in the food business. "Everyone told me it would be a wonderful experience. They told me I would love it. But I wanted to trade the certificate for something else, maybe in human services."

She enrolled for the first semester but soon had some problems at school and at home. For one thing, she was working part-time at Rosie's and couldn't get good day care. For another, the curriculum was not in line with her interests. What Tiara learned at Rosie's was professionalism—not a love for the food business. Also, because she was visually impaired, she couldn't see the blackboard. As a result, she was always playing catch-up after school to get what she missed during class.

"I explained to Rosie's that my family, my home, was in jeopardy. At that point I had some but not all of my kids back with me. I had to give up one or the other. And then it came to the point where I even had to choose between my home, my job, and my kids.

DSS said I was spending too much time outside and I didn't have the proper child care. I wasn't making enough money to pay anybody for babysitting because I wasn't working full-time."

Tiara dropped out of the culinary arts program. Although not openly criticized, she could feel the disappointment at Rosie's. To her, it felt as if she had let everyone down. "I tried to look at the big picture, and where they were coming from I can see I let them down. No one said anything, but I could feel it. They just felt I did not step up to the plate."

After she left the program, Tiara began to work at Rosie's full-time. By this time, she had all but two of her children out of foster care and back home. DSS told her she couldn't have the two youngest children unless she got better child care and stopped working weekends. The agency started talking to her about giving these two up for adoption.

"I was ready to settle for open adoption and keep my job and at least have visiting rights, so my kids would get to know who I was and I wouldn't be totally shut out. The person who had them said no to that arrangement. So I just said no to the adoption."

Because working weekends was an integral part of Tiara's job at Rosie's, she again had to make a choice. She went home and took care of her children.

"Now I'm ready to find a job again," she says. "I know there are things out there that I can do," She's applying for jobs, including one in a Boston hospital, and she has her family back together again. Every day she struggles to maintain her sobriety, knowing that is key to keeping herself together.

"I'm not a failure. I'm going to find something to pick me back up. So I keep going. I keep trying. If I have to keep asking the same people for another handout, I'll keep going. But I'm not going under. Life is like quicksand. It's up to you to keep afloat above the mud. You know you can float on water. It's mud that pulls you down."

6

THANKSGIVING

For 550 women in Boston, this Wednesday before Thanksgiving is a time to relax and be pampered, to eat well, to hear some music, and maybe even to dance a little. This afternoon, from sanctuaries all over the city, the women will converge on Rowes Wharf downtown. There they will board a ship and become guests at a holiday dinner Odyssey Cruise. The cruise around Boston Harbor, which is worth one hundred dollars, has been donated by the cruise line.

At Rosie's Place, several dozen women gather shortly before noon in the lobby outside the dining room to wait for the buses that will take them to Rowes Wharf. There are a few babies resting in the arms of their mothers, and a number of preschoolers who are zipping around, some climbing in and out of strollers. Almost as though a height limit has been imposed, there are no children taller than three feet or so. A sign on the door explains it: *Wednesday is a school day. School-aged children are not allowed on the Odyssey cruise.* Children are always welcome at Rosie's Place but not when they are old enough to be in school.

A few of the waiting women sink into the limited number of chairs that line the walls of the lobby.

The others stand, smoking cigarettes and talking. They keep looking out the door for their bus, but they are reluctant to venture into the chill air. Everyone shifts to make room for those who are snaking through the crowd to reach the dining room and lunch.

Finally the buses (painted to look like trolley cars) pull up in front. As they are climbing aboard, one woman asks the person next to her, "Do you think we're still getting a turkey today?" "Yeah," the woman answers. "When we get back from the cruise, they're supposed to be ready. My name's on the list—I *better* be getting one."

Thanksgiving turkeys and groceries are being assembled at Rosie's Place for those who will be making dinner somewhere the next day. Women wanting the food, like those interested in the cruise, must sign up a few days in advance. Along with the turkeys, there are vegetables and breads in the bags. For many of the women, a bag from Rosie's gives them an opportunity to contribute something to a dinner even if they aren't cooking the meal themselves. Others come to Rosie's Place for a big turkey dinner on Thanksgiving Day and then use the food over the long weekend.

The buses start and stop as they attempt to get through the crunch of holiday traffic. Some of the women are dozing as one small bus finally works its way to the wharf area and pulls up to the Boston

Harbor Hotel to let its passengers out. A nearby stand sells sweatshirts for forty-eight dollars.

"Forty-eight dollars!" one of the women exclaims. "Jesus, for forty-eight dollars you could get a really nice pair of warm boots." Her seatmate comments, "Tourists will pay anything. Who else would pay forty-eight dollars for something with writing on it that says 'Boston'?"

Once all the buses have arrived and the women have gotten off, there is another wait at the wharf to get on board the ship. With the sun ducking in and out of gathering clouds, it is cold down by the water. The women are edgy and shivering as they wait. Leaning up against a post, one woman finally calls out, "Can we *go,* already?"

A man in a crisp white uniform announces that it's time to board, and the line of women starts up the long gangplank. Some of the women walk alone, but most walk with one or two others. The women with canes or walkers come along last, helped by other women to manage the few steps. Uniformed crew members greet the women cheerily at the entrance to the ship. Everyone, from the staff who pilot and run the ship to the serving staff in the dining room, has volunteered to be here today. It is the second year this free dinner cruise has been offered to needy women.

The mood among the women lifts noticeably once they are on board, out of the cutting wind. There is a collective sigh of relief when the ship pulls away from the wharf—as though letting go of the mooring has helped everyone to let go of their worries.

The long tables are set with silverware and water glasses on white tablecloths. Friendly waiters and waitresses come around to take drink orders. No alcohol is offered, but the list of options is long. They repeat it, patiently, several times around each table.

All the waiters and waitresses are working outside their usual professions. After today, they will return to working as local politicians or writers and reporters from newspapers and television or radio stations. Their names are familiar to some of the passengers, who get a kick out of discovering these people waiting on tables instead of reading the news on the radio, writing a column for a newspaper, or appearing on television (as some of them still will that night). The attitude is uniformly upbeat. Cheerleaders from the New England Patriots, the local football team, are circulating throughout the decks.

~

The day before Thanksgiving is, for many women, a time of preparation and remembrance. There are memories of all the Thanksgivings that have preceded it—memories of baking or cleaning house or traveling by car to a relative's house or feeling a little frantic because there is too much to do. There is sometimes the bitter taste of problems that won't go away just because it's a holiday.

For Lauren, sitting on board the ship at a table marked "Rosie's Place," this day before Thanksgiving is her sixth clean day in a row—an endless, restless day that will, if she can pull it off, precede a seventh sober day.

Lauren is an overnight guest at Rosie's Place. Without naming the drug, she talks about how she has been sober for almost a week. She plays with her straight brown hair as she talks. Her dark blue eyes are guarded, avoiding contact with others.

Continuing a conversation begun on the bus with a woman whose baby was a crib death victim, Lauren talks about her own infant son who died four years earlier. Another woman at the table tells of her child who drowned. In less than an hour of sitting together, there has been talk about three baby boys dying. Once talking starts in earnest, losses are a common element.

The waitress for the table, host of a local television show, is on the run with one request after another. Lauren is demanding; she wants the waitress's complete attention all the time. She orders a Coke. She asks for a Shirley Temple. She orders a nonalcoholic Piña Colada. After that, it's bread. When the bread doesn't arrive fast enough, Lauren tugs on the waitress's sleeve again and repeats the request.

A friendly, round-faced, dark-suited man with glasses stops by to say hello. Lauren ignores him until she is told he's the mayor of Boston, and then she jumps up to pose for a picture with him. Mayor Tom Menino is happy to comply.

The meal is served: light and dark meat turkey with stuffing, lumpy mashed potatoes, squash, broccoli, cranberry sauce, and a large roll. When the plates are put down, Lauren says to the woman next to her, "If you're not going to eat that squash, I'll take it."

As dessert is offered—apple pie, pumpkin pie, and cheesecake—two New England Patriots cheerleaders sit down to talk with the women at the table. Lauren joins in immediately, turning the conversation around to herself. Her pale cheeks flush pink; she is energized by the cheerleaders' vibrant demeanor.

"I weighed ninety-seven pounds until I went to jail," Lauren tells them, apparently weighing about thirty or forty pounds more now. She doesn't say a word about how she happened to go to prison.

"Oh, my family has tons and tons of money," she says. "They cut me off because I was on drugs. They still hate me."

The two cheerleaders sit on either side of Lauren, forming a unit of three women in their early twenties. While Lauren keeps her coat on over her sweater and jeans, the two cheerleaders are dressed in matching blue-and-white outfits with short skirts and short tight jackets, their well-exposed legs encased in shiny pantyhose. They have applied their makeup in the same way, and they wear their hair in the same style, long, curly, and well moussed.

They listen as Lauren tells about her struggle with addiction.

Lauren has been trying without success to get into a detox program. Now she is attempting to get clean on her own. Temptation is everywhere. "When I wanted drugs," she says, "no one wanted to give me any. Now that I don't, everyone is trying to get me to take something."

One of the cheerleaders tells her, "You need to have a positive attitude and regain your family's trust. Have you told them you're clean?"

"Well, I've been clean a thousand times, and they don't really trust me now."

"You can do it," the cheerleaders tell her, repeatedly.

Lauren tells them that they are the best-looking cheerleaders in the group. "You are the two most beautiful ones," she says. Hoping she has found a couple of new friends, she asks for their home telephone numbers. One of the women says she lives with her father; the other says she lives with her mother, that she doesn't have her own phone.

Lauren gives them her phone number at Rosie's. She tells them how she ran into a former friend a few days earlier and the woman had asked her where she was living. Lauren rolls her eyes and then covers her face with her hands. "I was so embarrassed," she says softly.

"That's nothing to be ashamed of!" one of the cheerleaders responds.

"Oh, but it is. It really is," Lauren says, lifting her head up defiantly.

~

DURING THE TWO-HOUR CRUISE, the ship slowly travels around Boston Harbor, passing the tall buildings of the financial district, the runways of Logan Airport, and Castle Island; it is never far from shore. The weather, initially off-and-on sunny, has settled on cloudy, and the first snowfall of the year begins. As the ship goes north along the coastline, the flakes fall thick and white but not heavy enough to obscure the view.

Below deck, everyone waits for the entertainment to start. At the Rosie's Place table, Sarah Rose talks about how she is moving into a new apartment on the first of the month. She is, as always, full of news about what's going on in Rosie's clothing room, where she volunteers.

"Did you hear how someone donated a full-length mink coat?" she asks. "Still had the tags on it—three thousand dollars! I tried it on. I loved it—but who could wear a coat like that? Anyone who tried to wear it would get robbed in fifteen minutes."

So what happened to the coat? Everyone wants to know. "Oh, it was donated somewhere; someone on staff found a place for it."

Finally, the cheerleaders get up to perform. They do three identical dance numbers on two decks. The crowd goes wild. Several women are having such a good time that they start jumping up and down, spurred on by the music and the example being set by the cheerleaders.

After the dance numbers have ended, a drummer and a keyboard player accompany a young singer named Dawn on the upper deck. Dawn gives the microphone to a seventyish black woman from Rosie's Place. In a style reminiscent of Aretha Franklin, the woman does a couple of songs made popular by the Beatles. There is an escalating wave of whistles and clapping.

"Give me money, that's what I want." She belts it out. The audience is with her. When she starts in on "Give me some rock 'n' roll music," several small boys start dancing. A radio newscaster familiar to early-morning listeners in the Boston area takes the hands of a little girl from Rosie's, and they dance together.

There is some down time as the ship heads south, back to the wharf. Women with young children tend to them, and babies are passed around to be cuddled. Some women go up to the cold outer deck for cigarettes, since the dining areas are smoke-free. Other women simply wait, looking bored or just exhausted. No one is looking at the view anymore.

The women from 437, a permanent residence that guests of Rosie's may apply for, remain seated at one of the long tables with Katherine Goodwin, their house manager. Unlike many of the tables, where there is noise and constant motion, this one is characterized by a quiet hum. The women seem comfortable with each other and continue to chat as the ship slowly makes its way back to the dock. Having just finished one Thanksgiving dinner, the women at this table are busily planning the one they will prepare the next day in their own home.

~

"I hope I'm never tested the way the women here have been," Katherine Goodwin says. "Would I be as strong and as smart and survive the way they have?"

Katherine lives and works at 437. It is one of three permanent residences that are not physically attached to the main Rosie's Place building but are connected by staff, services, and philosophy. To the twelve women living at 437, this narrow, high-ceilinged, brick row house is home for as long as they need it.

When she has paperwork or phone calls, Katherine can be found in her office on the third floor, typically dressed in a flannel shirt and casual pants, with her light brown hair pulled back by a headband or barrettes. She keeps the door open, choosing to face the life of the house rather than the busy street and tall buildings that can be seen out the window.

The women at 437 range in age from early thirties to late seventies. Each woman has her own bedroom and shares a living room, kitchen, and bathroom with the other tenants. Although the women may cook here, some choose to eat lunch and dinner at Rosie's, or "The Big House." They may go over to Rosie's because their friends are there or because they want to keep in touch with volunteers who work particular shifts. One resident never cooks or buys groceries, so she eats at Rosie's all the time; another eats at Rosie's only when money is short at the end of the month.

Most of the women, however, choose to cook for themselves in the kitchen at 437. Sometimes two women will agree that the one who doesn't mind running errands will get the food and the other will do the cooking. Sometimes, when a car or van is not available, a staff member will help a woman with grocery shopping.

"There are some good cooks living here," Katherine says. "When I'm up in my office, I leave the door open so the women don't have to come all the way up the stairs but can just give a yell. Sometimes when the women are cooking, I say, 'I'm gaining weight just smelling it.'"

There's a rhythm to the evenings at 437. Most of the women finish dinner by 7:00. After that, they usually sit together in the bay-windowed living room on the first floor and watch a couple of game shows. "Jeopardy" is a favorite.

"God, they're good at those shows," Katherine marvels. "It doesn't matter what the women are dealing with—whether it's physical or mental health problems or substance addiction—the women are all so sharp. Some people seem to think if you have a mental health problem you're retarded. That's a problem in itself."

By the time a woman ends up at Rosie's Place, she has usually run out of choices. According to Katherine, "Usually a woman's here because she doesn't have family support. Or she may simply have burned out the family because of substance abuse or mental health problems." Katherine has worked at Rosie's Place for ten years. At least half of the women at 437 have been there for three or four years, and one woman began living there a year before Katherine arrived. The policy is that women can stay for as long or as short a period of time as they need.

The women need varying amounts of support. Some have full-time jobs and need little or no help from the staff. Some work and pay a small rent until they can accumulate enough money to move into their own place. All of them pay 30 percent of their income as rent, whether they have a job or are on some kind of government assistance. They are given free use of two washers, two dryers, and laundry soap. Because they live at 437, they can go with Katherine to Rosie's and pick up clothing when they need it. Katherine explains: "If a woman is working full-time for six or seven dollars an hour, she's not making a living wage. Even working eight hours a day, she can't afford a safe apartment, so 437 is a solution that could work well for her."

There are two studio apartments with a shared kitchen on the top floor of 437. The two women who live there have more privacy than those who live on the lower floors, but they have to climb five flights of stairs to get to it. "We say we have a cheap Stairmaster; you don't have to pay a hundred dollars every month to go to a gym," Katherine says of the floor where she lived as a part-time staff member when she arrived at Rosie's. "I live down in the basement now and realize how much lighter and healthier I was when I lived up there. You don't tend to carry a lot of groceries up five flights of stairs."

Few of the women at 437 tell people they are living at a Rosie's Place lodging house. They know the label *homeless* can be translated, somehow, as *temporary* or even *crazy.* "The women don't want that stigma attached. This is where they live. This isn't a home for battered women; this isn't a home for crazy people. This is a home," Katherine says.

In many ways, the occupants of 437 are an extended family. Katherine is a member of the staff, but she is also the mother of two grown daughters, who have come many times to visit. It is the women themselves who keep Katherine at Rosie's. She enjoys meeting the constant challenge of reaching out to find common ground. She has yet to run across a woman at 437 that she cannot connect with—she just needs the chance to know each woman well enough to find that little piece that makes the connection. "We all want to be cared about. We all want people to like us. That's always the most exciting part for me, the finding of that little piece."

It's exciting, but it's not easy. A tenant may be withdrawn or angry. She may be a little intimidating to everyone, not just the staff. In that case, Katherine sits back and waits, watching and listening.

~

This kind of work was never part of Katherine's life plan. If she had been told twenty years ago that she would be working at a Rosie's Place residence, she would not have believed it.

Married at eighteen, Katherine had two children by the time she was twenty. She and her husband, a college dean, lived in upstate New York. When her daughters were young, she stayed home as a full-time mother. When they were in middle school, she started working part-time jobs that fit into their schedule. More than anything else, the clerical work Katherine did during this time helped her to decide what she did *not* want to do. She was hungry for something more challenging.

When one of her daughters was in college, Katherine spent a week in the dormitory with her. She slept on the floor and went to some of the classes. "I couldn't believe it!" Katherine recalls. "I knew it all! I said, 'I can do this!' It was eye-opening for me." By the time both of her daughters were finishing college, Katherine had applied to Mount Holyoke College in western Massachusetts. Using retirement money from her job, scholarships, and student loans, she enrolled full-time as one of sixty women in Mount Holyoke's program for older women. The women in the program ranged in age from twenty-three to sixty-eight.

Though she was married, Katherine moved into a dormitory. She didn't want to take classes during the day and be a housewife at night. She wanted, instead, to come as close as she could to the complete college experience of being on her own for the first time. To do so in a freshman dorm, Katherine made it clear right away that, as she put it, "I'm not anybody's mother." She found living on campus liberating. She majored in politics, minored in women's studies, and as part of a work/study program, worked in a family shelter in Northampton.

Around the time Katherine graduated, her marriage broke up, and she had to decide where to live as well as where to work. The abuse she had seen at the Northampton family shelter gave an added dimension to her minor in women's studies. She knew she was interested in working with women. "I realized I had absolutely no energy for support for men because there were plenty of places out there that were taking care of the men." Katherine's feelings mirrored those of Kip Tiernan, who had started Rosie's Place, at least in part, in response to seeing women disguising themselves as men to get meals and shelter.

The director of the Northampton shelter told Katherine that if she was considering living in Boston, the best place to work with women was Rosie's Place. As it happened, the newspaper was advertising a position at Rosie's. Katherine applied for the job and got it.

As a part-time staffer with housing provided, Katherine's job was for her to be available to the residents of 437 in the evening for emergencies. She moved into one of the fifth-floor studio apartments. Altogether, five staff members were working in the house, and three of them were living there. An intercom system connected all the rooms.

"We needed to address all kinds of issues, including serious mental health problems. We had to be active advocates and say to the women, 'I will work with you every single day. If you will get the help you need, we will guarantee the support.'"

While Katherine offered to back up the women, sometimes the women needed to help *her* out. She had never lived in a city, and she didn't know anyone. "What was so wonderful was that the women recognized that living in the city, I was totally out of my element. As far as taking care of myself and being safe, I knew nothing." At one point, Katherine recalls, the residents sat her down in the living room and said she had taken a big risk by walking home from downtown after dark. "They told me what buses to take and when to take them and when not to; they let me know what subway stops were okay and where not to go. I'm supposed to be here supporting the women—but that has been my experience, living and working here, that it works the other way around."

As the white manager of a house made up predominantly of women of color, Katherine has learned that stereotypes work both ways. People discriminate; everyone makes assumptions. One of the clearest examples of this happened a few years ago when Katherine and a black woman in the house were trading stories of childhood experiences. Each woman, they discovered, had grown up in a working-class family with a mother, a father, a grandmother, brothers, and sisters all sharing the same space. There were problems, but there were also tremendous advantages in the crowded but close living situation. The two women found there were many more similarities in their living experiences than differences.

"It was as if she were talking about my life," Katherine says. "When she realized I had shared the same upbringing, she left all that 'You're a white woman—you don't understand' behind."

As a staff member, Katherine is an advocate, helping women to deal with the procedures that will get them what they need, whether it is scheduling and getting to routine medical appointments or interacting with bureaucracies, such as Social Security or welfare. Medical emergencies are also a part of her work. Every day is different. Sometimes her most important job is just to be there as a friend.

"One of the women needed something at Filene's department store. As a black woman, she had never had a positive experience downtown. She walked with her head down, trying not to be noticed. When I went with her, I slipped my arm through hers—we were just friends together, out shopping. We were comfortable together, but I was aware that she was treated with more respect, unfortunately, just because she was with me."

Being one of twelve children, Katherine believes, is the key to her concept of living in a community. She grew up with two parents who worked and a grandmother who was at home for the children. The large family had a complicated system for handling household chores that kept everything on track. "My father was very vocal, but my mother was the true strength of the family. When I look back on it, it took a tremendous amount of organization on my mother's part, working full-time and having twelve kids. My mother insisted that we always sit down together at a meal."

Everyone helped out, even the youngest children, and everyone had some kind of job to do. Doing the job made every member of the family feel valued because he or she was contributing something for the good of the household. "I try to apply that here. You have to be realistic, this is a community setting. There are staff members here to offer the support that's needed, which may be something different for each woman in the house. We don't expect the women to be best friends, but we do expect them to be respectful. When we have activities that bring the women together, when they've laughed or kidded around with each other, it's harder to be angry when someone later just rubs them the wrong way. And of course we rub each other the wrong way sometimes. It's a case of getting to know the person as a human being. It's harder to be angry at someone after you've heard them talk about an experience you've also shared."

~

LIFE AT 437 IS CALM on this Thanksgiving Day, and the women are doing the cooking as a group. Every year, at the monthly house meetings in September and October, part of the agenda is to discuss the holidays—and every year since Katherine has been there, the consensus has been to have Thanksgiving together at 437. From the outside, the building with its eight steps leading up to the front door looks like every other building on the block. Behind the door and downstairs, snuggled in under the steps, however, the scent of Thanksgiving emanates from Katherine's basement apartment, where she stuffs, bastes, and roasts the holiday turkey. When it's ready, she calls for one of the women to come down and help her lug the twenty-pound bird up to the dining room for carving.

As in most homes, cooking goes on here every day, and as in most homes, Thanksgiving Day is different. This is one mealtime no one watches television. By pushing two or three tables together, there's room for everyone to sit down together. The women get out the Thanksgiving decorations, the china, a tablecloth reserved for special occasions, pretty napkins, and fresh flowers.

Together, in the early afternoon, they put the food on the table. Several of the women contribute a dish of their choice, which they have prepared themselves. Included are fantastic sweet potatoes made with apple cider, and a few Southern dishes that several women remember from their childhoods—collard greens, black beans and rice. Everyone contributes in some way, if not by cooking, then by setting the table or cleaning up afterwards. For many of the women, part of the enjoyment is taking care of each other on the holiday. They take pleasure in being able to do this, since they are usually not in a position to take care of others.

"We always have too much food! And that's part of it. We have enough for leftovers all weekend," Katherine says with a smile. After dinner, they talk, telling stories as the light dims into dusk and nighttime. "We end up laughing our heads off. Sometimes it's a matter of laughing so you don't cry. What we're doing is sharing."

Like any family, this family of women talk about things they have seen on the television news or read about in the newspapers, but soon the conversation turns to the personal, and they share memories from years before. Shared stories come from family relationships, the experience of being someone's child or someone's mother.

For Katherine, holidays have always been times for sharing. When she was growing up, her parents worked in a hospital for epileptics. Her mother brought home children who didn't have anywhere else to go for the holidays. "There was nothing wrong with the children," Katherine remembers, "except they sometimes had seizures. We now know better, but back then it was a terrible stigma for a family to have a child with epilepsy. Some people were in the hospital for life. Their parents dropped them off there and never tried to see them again.

"I didn't realize at the time what my mother was doing for these children, giving them the experience of just being kids in a regular home for the holiday. There were babies through teenagers who came, and to us they were ordinary, like anybody else. It was always kind of crazy at our house anyway, with a dozen kids in the family."

Not every Thanksgiving at 437 has been as mellow as this one. Some holidays, Katherine notes, are more successful than others, depending on what is going on in the house. Earlier in the life of 437, she recalls, "the staff was just trying to keep the women from hurting each other or themselves. We recognized we needed to address the reasons the women became homeless." Now, the staff tries to head off serious problems by making sure support systems are in place before a woman moves in. The entire staff does its best to avoid putting the other women at risk.

"There might be someone who's acting out, and the better you get to know her, the more you understand the reasons for it. Sometimes you have to be firm about something and set boundaries, even to the point of saying she is putting her housing at risk. Then later that afternoon or the next day she will say or do something that makes you just laugh. She begins to see that she is cared about as an individual, so trust is beginning to be built, trust that she can act out and not be thrown out totally."

Katherine knows for a fact that this is the first holiday some of the women in the house have ever celebrated in the way that many people assume is traditional. Living lives marked by a lack of choices, these women are choosing to spend their Thanksgiving with a traditional turkey dinner and the people who constitute their family at 437. Katherine concludes simply, "There have been a number of miracles throughout my experience at Rosie's."

7

CHRISTMAS DAY

"Will you shut up?!" Garnet, a Rosie's Place guest, screams, her usual elegant demeanor and beaming smile lost for the moment. Garnet is heavily invested in the drama of a Bingo game. Thumping her cane on the floor, she is alternately elated and annoyed, yelling at anyone who dares hamper her ability to hear the numbers. In front of her is a teetering stack of Bingo markers. She has already won a dozen prizes, including several pieces of jewelry—she is on a roll. She leans over the assortment protectively as she scans her card. Suddenly, she's half out of her chair.

"B-3! B-3! B-3! Yes! Yes!" One of the volunteers hands Garnet a bracelet, and she adds it to her pile of winnings before turning her attention to the new game. Around her, several dining room tables are filled with women who sit quietly picking at muffins and sipping coffee while concentrating on their Bingo cards as the numbers are read.

Christmas Day brunch at Rosie's begins at 10:00 with volunteers cooking eggs and French toast at the big kitchen stoves. They fill and refill huge platters of fresh fruit and pastries. The number of volunteers grows steadily as the morning wears on. When there are momentary lulls in the activities, some of the volunteers lean against the back counter, arms folded, with nothing to do. Some chat; others are munching on bread, straightening up, and replacing food on the trays as needed.

Christmas Day volunteers work steadily throughout the morning as runners, cooks, assistant cooks, and clean-up personnel. Runners bring up small slips of paper with orders for eggs from guests at the tables. Breakfast cooks, mostly men dressed in their own Rosie's Place red volunteer aprons or in white ones borrowed from the supply drawer, are busy at the stoves until noon. They fry and scramble eggs as the slips of paper appear in the kitchen.

At noon, the volunteers swarm around, cleaning tables, washing dishes, cutting up vegetables. They are dressed in varying degrees of formality, from jeans and sweaters to dresses, though most are wearing casual clothes. Holidays at Rosie's are notable for the sheer numbers of volunteers. They come mostly in the form of family groups and adult mother-daughter duos. Today includes one mother with her three preteenage girls. Some of the volunteers have never been here before. Some come because they don't celebrate the holiday themselves and it gives them a place to go. Many come simply because they like to do a generous deed on Christmas Day.

Santia Robinson, one of Rosie's guests, walks up to the counter. She is a short, handsome woman wearing a tailored black sweater trimmed in red and a wig with corn rows. She has been coming in a lot for lunch lately, usually with four little girls trailing behind. This time Santia is alone.

"Where are your kids today? Didn't you bring them?" asks one of the regular volunteers as she gets a plate ready and hands it to Santia.

"No, I was supposed to, but I don't have them," she answers, her broad, intelligent face reflecting a bone-deep weariness. She takes her plate over to a table along the wall and sits down.

THE FOUR SMILING LITTLE GIRLS who often accompany Santia are her grandchildren, beautiful youngsters with round faces in varying shades of brown. All bear a remarkable resemblance to her. When people point this out, as they are apt to do, Santia laughs and agrees. "I don't know how it happened, but every one of my grands looks just like me!"

Santia's only child is Martin. He is thirty-one years old and has more than a dozen children by four women. He lives in a neighboring state now, but all his children live with their mothers, and all of them live within a few blocks of each other and Santia—in Roxbury, a part of Boston adjacent to the South End neighborhood that is home to Rosie's.

For Santia, the week preceding Christmas started with a desperate call from Adrienne, the mother of eight of Martin's children. Adrienne didn't know what she was going to do about Christmas for the kids, Santia explains to the regular volunteer who has joined her briefly at the table. There was no food in the house and no presents, and she was in a panic. Santia responded immediately. "I tried every shelter to get gifts for the kids. I went around to every place I could go. It's just not right, for kids not to have any gifts for Christmas."

All week Santia rounded up presents wherever they were giving them out, including Rosie's, and she found something for each one of her grandchildren. She borrowed some money from a friend to buy food for Christmas dinner. By Christmas Eve, she was all set. She got on the phone to Adrienne to find out what time they could get together.

"Oh, we're not going to be here," Adrienne said. "We're going up to Christmasland in New Hampshire for the day."

Santia had never heard of Christmasland, and she could tell by the sound of Adrienne's voice that she had been smoking crack. This scenario is gruesomely familiar to Santia. She has taken care of the children many times when Adrienne can't handle them. Five-year-old Debbie was born twitching and screaming, a crack baby, and Santia took care of her at that time.

Adrienne has gone into detox several times, Santia explains. A few years ago, when there were not as many children as there are now, the kids stayed at Santia's apartment while Adrienne was in detox. Now there are just too many children for Santia to keep with her. She can't handle more than a few at a time, and as much as she desperately wants to help, there isn't room for any more in her tiny apartment. "I only have four chairs," she says.

Santia's initial disappointment over the Christmas Eve situation gave way to rage and eventually to fatigue at this latest episode in a series of backslides on Adrienne's part. Santia knew she could not give in to her anger and chastise Adrienne. It just wouldn't help the ones who are being hurt the most.

"Mad as I am," she explains to the volunteer, "I know if I give the mother a really hard time I'll never get to see the kids. They need me. I don't give money to Martin any more—I've learned that—but the kids need so much, everything really. What else can I do, except keep trying to help where I can?"

So on this Christmas afternoon, she has put on a red-trimmed sweater and made her way over to Rosie's alone. "I never got to cook the food I bought, and I wasn't doing anything. I thought I might as well come over for dinner. I always find myself coming back here."

~

Santia works for the Massachusetts Society for the Prevention of Cruelty to Children (MSPCC), an organization housed in a beige art deco building in Boston's South End. Before it became home to the MSPCC, the building was Morgan Memorial, the center of Boston's Salvation Army operation. Santia's job is to go into homes, check on how the kids are doing, talk to the parents, and make reports. The walls of the office that she shares with two other caseworkers are covered with children's drawings. Santia doesn't get to enjoy the drawings often, however; most of the time she needs to be out in the field.

Santia's job echoes her life. Both present the same kinds of problems inherent in caring for children while having too few resources, and in dealing with adults who cannot be good parents. At work, Santia is a smart, capable woman who does her job and is compensated for it. This part of her life is well defined—she gets a paycheck, she does the work she believes in, and unlike her home life, there is a cutoff point; she is out of there at the end of the day.

"My work is my salvation," she says.

The job requires a lot of physical activity. Santia must travel around the city, climb up and down stairs, and pick up toddlers. Last summer, on a work assignment, she fell on some steps and hurt her knee. Since then, she has had to take a lot of time off—a situation that is particularly frustrating to her now, during the Christmas season. Her knee aches constantly and frequently buckles under her weight. As she needs to be able to get to where her clients live, which is often up several flights of stairs, she doesn't know when she will be able to go back to her job.

For years, Santia has brought her grandchildren on the bus to Rosie's for meals, especially lunches. When she can, she brings Adrienne's four little girls—Debbie, Kyla, and the twins, Tenice and Sylvia. Santia sees these trips to Rosie's as an opportunity to teach her grandchildren how to function out in the world. She corrects their table manners, speech, and behavior. At the same time, she loves to joke around with the girls—they know she can find a funny side to almost anything. They are respectful to Grandma Santia. She is their anchor, a provider of stability even when she is uncertain about how she is going to take care of herself.

~

Santia was born when her mother, Ilana, was eighteen and living in North Carolina. She was Ilana's third baby. When Santia was three months old, Ilana gave her to her great-aunt Juanita in Virginia to raise.

As a small child, Santia never saw her mother. People did tell her she had older and younger sisters and brothers living somewhere. "No one ever tried to hide my mother's name. I knew what it was, but I never had a face to go with it, so it didn't mean much to me." Santia never knew who her father was.

She grew up surrounded by cousins, the grandchildren of her great-aunt and great-uncle. Aunt

Juanita and Uncle Gerard were "very religious, Bible-thumping people, but they loved the hell out of me. My aunt was the type who would take anybody's baby and watch over it. Why, she even took the neighbor's child in."

There were other heroes in Santia's childhood, including a godmother who was kind to her, providing her with clothing and taking her on outings. Growing up, Santia went to her godmother's house every Christmas. Her godmother was a gospel singer who toured all over the country and brought Santia gifts from her travels. "She took me to see Mahalia Jackson when I was five. I didn't know who I was lookin' at then!" Santia remembers, shaking her head at her own innocence.

When she was seven, Santia was taken to see her mother, who was living in another city. "Someone said, 'That's your mother!' and I couldn't imagine she was right there in front of me, and I said, 'That's *not* my mother.'" According to Santia, an argument followed and Ilana told Great-Aunt Juanita that she had to give Santia back. Juanita held firm, saying that the child's place was with her since she had never lived in any other family.

It wasn't until four years later that Ilana's threat to take Santia back became more real. By that time, Ilana had already moved closer to Juanita and had said that she was coming back for her child. Ilana had several more children by then, and she was drinking. She would come around to the house and harass Juanita about Santia's custody. Santia wanted to stay with her great-aunt, who was the only mother she had ever known.

"I realize now it wasn't my problem, it was my mother's problem," Santia says. "But I didn't want to hurt my great-aunt, and I didn't want my mother to hurt her either. I was doing well in school and they trusted the honor-roll kids to a certain extent, but I took advantage of this and started running away when I could."

Finally, the custody case went to court. The judge asked Santia whom she wanted to live with, her great-aunt or her mother. Her mother was sitting in the courtroom looking at her, and Santia said, "I'll go live with my mother." Now, more than thirty years later, she points out that she did not say, "I *want* to live with my mother." Santia felt she had to go with her biological mother. She wasn't even sure her great-aunt would take her back at that point, since she had turned into a chronic runaway.

Through all of this, Santia maintained good grades. The mothers of her friends sometimes helped her out. "One of my friend's mothers even gave me bus fare to leave because she knew what was going on at home." They saw that she was a good kid, still a preteen, caught in a bad situation.

Looking back, Santia says, "I don't know why my mother wanted me back. She was living a bad lifestyle. No one even checked her police record before they sent me back to live with her." Prior to the custody case, Ilana had been charged with attempted murder. She had gotten off, but Santia feels that if anyone had known, they wouldn't have let Ilana have Santia. When Ilana later beat a woman with a high-heeled shoe, she was sent to a women's prison for a year, and the children were scattered once again.

"That's why I'm so hung up on my grandchildren staying together," Santia says.

~

Santia was in ninth grade when she found out she was pregnant, so naive that she didn't even know how she had conceived. When Martin was born, fifteen-year-old Santia took her baby to the only place she considered her true home—Auntie Juanita's house.

A few years later, Santia's mother moved to Boston. Santia, who had been struggling to support herself and get a life together for her son, let Martin go live with his grandmother. Santia followed them north and took Martin back when he was in elementary school.

As Martin grew older, he became unruly. Boston offered temptations he found hard to resist, and he started getting into trouble. "By the time Martin was ten or eleven and until he was thirteen years old," Santia recalls, "he was having trouble in school. They deemed him incorrigible, and I had no idea what I was going to do with him." Finally, a minister helped Santia get Martin into a private school in New Hampshire. Martin came home on weekends. For the first time in years, the boy was doing well in school, and he seemed to enjoy being there. Santia relaxed.

Before Martin could graduate, however, the school was closed. Santia never knew why. Martin returned to Roxbury High School, as tough an urban environment as a kid can encounter. Although he had been a National Honor Society candidate at the New Hampshire private school, he was put into classes at Roxbury that didn't challenge him, and he began to skip school. He ended up in juvenile court, arrested for breaking and entering.

"By the time he was eighteen, women started having babies for him," Santia says. The oldest child is now in middle school.

Santia sometimes slips and refers to Martin as "my baby." When she sends Christmas cards, they are signed "Santia and Martin." She picked out clothes for him until he was well into his twenties. "Everyone wanted to know where he got them, too. He always looked good," she beams.

~

For many women at Rosie's, the biggest problem is isolation, lack of family. For Santia, on the other hand, the dynamics of her family always threaten to pull her down as she struggles to improve her life. She is always the helper, seldom the one who is helped. Her relationship with her mother continues to be troubled, and for years she has been heavily involved with the needs of her grandchildren, their mothers, and Martin. Santia also deals with her large family of half-siblings, whom she didn't know until the custody battle when she was a preteen. Most of these half-siblings moved to Boston when Ilana did and now live in the neighborhood near Rosie's Place.

About a year ago, Santia's oldest brother, Warren, was stabbed to death by her youngest brother, Parker, in their mother's house. When Santia and Warren were younger, he was hard on her, but as the two of them got older, they grew to respect each other and became friends. "I found out I could have conversations with him," Santia says sadly.

It was Santia's niece who came to her door to tell her about the murder hours after it happened. The next day the story was in the local papers and television news. Warren, who was forty-eight years old and still lived at home, had been upstairs in his room, working with his computer and his music. He worked for a local cable station and made videos of neighborhood events and weddings as a business. Parker, who was thirty-nine and out on parole from a prison in the Midwest, had been staying at Ilana's house for about two weeks. According to Santia's niece, Parker had gone upstairs to see Warren. After a minute or two, Ilana heard a thump, and then Parker came downstairs and said, "I told you I was going to kill him." Ilana ran upstairs as fast as she could.

"When my mother got to the door of the room," relates Santia, "she saw my brother wearing just a pair of boxer shorts, with his head in a puddle of blood. Parker had cut him; that's how he did it."

Ilana's sister, who was upstairs in the house, called 911. The ambulance came and took Warren away. After a long afternoon of waiting, Ilana called the hospital to check on Warren's condition. She finally reached a nurse and was told her son was dead. "Oh, didn't you know how bad he was?" the nurse asked her.

"Nobody knows what really happened," says Santia. "Everyone said Parker had been acting crazy the last couple of weeks. I guess they were arguing, but Warren was very soft-spoken, and no one heard him say anything that day. It has never taken much to set Parker off. Short fuses just go off."

For Santia, who was still grieving over the death of her very favorite brother, Raymond, Warren's death has been a nightmare. "Raymond and I used to have so much fun together. We danced all the time. Hey, we even won dance contests. Those were good days," she says. Raymond died of AIDS in prison. Santia says she did not know he had the virus until it was too late and didn't get to see him. "People kept telling me he was out of prison because he kept getting pneumonia. I should have known, but I didn't," she sighs.

"Pretty soon all the boys in the family will be gone. Warren was taken out. Parker was taken away."

Santia is afraid Parker will commit suicide when remorse sinks in, as she is sure it will. She also worries about Martin, even though he is in his thirties. It isn't only run-ins with the law that trouble her. "All those women in his life! I'm just afraid one of them is going to cut him one of these days, and that he's going to come home to me in a box."

Over the years, Santia has been in and out of work, off-and-on homeless. She has taken advantage of the meals, counseling, clothing, and rent assistance offered by Rosie's Place. At times, when she has needed to, she has stayed overnight.

One of the women who has helped Santia when she has needed it most, obviously impressed with her resiliency, is the director of a mental health agency. "She has saved me, I'm not kidding, many different times—given me work, taken me to her vacation place, helped me figure out my direction in life. She always told me I could get where I wanted to go, and she helped me find a way," Santia says. "A lot of times just talking on the phone helps."

~

In counterpoint to Santia's story, the mood at Rosie's on Christmas Day is light. It may be the holiday extras—the decorations and packages—or possibly the abundance of food that is being served nonstop. Children buzz around. Gifts for women and kids have been flowing all week. Some of the presents come from bulk donations; some are purchased by staff and volunteers for specific children.

Conversations ebb and flow throughout the dining room. Guests talk to guests; regular volunteers from Wednesday dinners meet the Friday lunch crew; Sunday night caterers get to know the people who come every other Tuesday. Many conversations begin, "What shift do you usually work? How long have you been coming here?"

After the guests have eaten their roast beef dinners, it's time to get the dessert out. Two or three volunteers break away from the gang in the kitchen to go into the dining room with bowls of rice pudding. A tall woman with a long brown ponytail arrives at Santia's table with a large metal tray. The woman tips the tray so Santia can have a look at all the choices. Santia looks over the selection and picks one with a good crop of raisins.

Until Santia has knee surgery, she can't consistently work at the job she loves. She has been offered and has accepted a temporary job filling in for a receptionist at a therapy clinic. She'll get some much-needed money from that. "It will get me used to working again. It will be good. That's what happened last time—I was hired as a receptionist and I was moved into a better job. They saw my potential. They said I was doing more good for people out in the waiting room than when they went inside for therapy," she chuckles.

Now, scraping the pudding bowl, thoughtful in her Christmas sweater, Santia says, "Rosie's has always been here for me. I walked right by my mother's house to get here. I know I always have a place here, even when my own mother can't help me."

AFTERWORD

WHEN KIP TIERNAN OPENED Rosie's Place, it was a storefront with a coffeepot, sandwiches, flowers, and music. Today, more than twenty years later, it serves close to 6000 meals a month, employs 41 people, enjoys the help of a core group of about 350 volunteers, and has a $2 million budget. Rosie's Place now is organized as a corporation of 93 members with an 18-member board of directors. It engages in ongoing fund-raising activities in and around Boston and can, therefore, offer a wide range of programming and an always growing array of services for women. What has not changed at all is the philosophy of Rosie's Place—to accept all women unconditionally and nonjudgmentally.

"As an organization, we have never gotten into systems-thinking; from the time women step in the door, they count," says Executive Director Julie Brandlen. "There are no pat answers, there is not an institutional approach, and we do not fall into 'that's not our policy'—all of which means there can be an answer. The challenge is how to make it work. We keep trying 250 times, if that's what it takes."

Still, Rosie's Place needs to constantly grow and change to keep up with the needs of the women, and that task gets more and more difficult. Welfare reform has meant that everyone involved with keeping Rosie's Place going needs to pedal ever faster.

"We have always needed to stretch, to think of ways we can help the women who come here. Now we need to stretch even more," Brandlen says.

Rosie's Place is filled to capacity every night now, with twenty women staying in the overnight program. Staff members help find beds for everyone who needs them in shelters scattered throughout the Roxbury and Dorchester areas of Boston. An additional thirty-two women are living at the other three houses connected with Rosie's Place, including the house for women living with HIV.

In an emergency, a woman who needs food can get groceries. A woman can get immediate financial help in order to pay a two-month rental deposit or an overdue utility bill before the heat is cut off. A woman can get placed in a substance addiction program or a mental health facility if she needs it, or she can get transportation back to her family if that is where she can get some support.

Every year, more than one hundred women move into their own homes thanks to Rosie's Place. Furniture is obtained through the Massachusetts Coalition for the Homeless. Pots and pans, flatware, sheets and towels, and similar items make up the several household orders that volunteers fill every week from donations.

An elder apartment has been set up at one of the Rosie's Place permanent residences to provide a home for women over the age of fifty-five who have intensive medical needs.

During Friday lunches, the New England Eye Institute sets up a miniclinic in the TV room off the dining room. As well as performing eye exams, the institute distributes almost two hundred pairs of glasses to Rosie's guests each year.

Rosie's Place also offers a chance to go back to school. The Joan R. Sawyer Scholarship Fund provides help with tuition for college, trade school, or special training. Volunteers come in to help women work on skills that will increase their chances of getting a job.

Last year, 224 women at Rosie's Place received legal assistance from the Shelter Legal Services Foundation, a nonprofit corporation that offers help to poor people. The foundation is made up of a director, 75 law students, and 60 practicing attorneys, most of them volunteers. A group comes to Rosie's every Monday night and gives advice on benefits problems and landlord relations, for instance, and on issues of family law, including child support, custody, and dealing with the state social service agency.

On Tuesday afternoons, a representative from the Boston Area Rape Crisis Center comes to meet with women who need counseling.

A representative from the Social Security Administration comes in once a week to counsel the women on what is available to them. The representative helps cut through the paperwork with its often bewildering forms.

The Rosie's Place Food Pantry has been in operation for a couple of years, currently supplying about 4000 bags of groceries to guests annually. Recently, the food pantry has been supplemented by a new service called Dollar Foods. The food, which is donated to poor people throughout the city, is delivered to Rosie's Place once a week. Women can place orders for the foods they wish—specifying categories such as breads, fresh fruits, or vegetables or requesting a combination of items—and then they pay one dollar per bag when they pick up the order. The first day of the program, thirty women signed up, and demand is growing fast.

Caterers, the volunteer groups that provide prepared meals, are the backbone of the food operation at Rosie's. The thirty-five caterers, who may be friends acting together or small groups or larger scale church efforts, each provide at least one meal per month. Some of the caterers have been coming to Rosie's Place for seventeen years.

Every week, the beauty salon is turned into a clinic when nursing students from Regis College come to Rosie's Place to provide on-site, one-on-one care. The nursing students do everything from soaking tired feet to conducting screenings of all kinds, including for tuberculosis. They administer flu shots; they educate the women about dental hygiene; and when needed, they accompany guests to medical appointments.

Rosie's Place is always on the lookout for innovative ways to help women help themselves. The Women's Craft Cooperative is a good example. In 1996, a student from nearby Lesley College approached Rosie's Place with the concept of putting together a craft business. It was implemented that same year. Although some of the materials are purchased, thousands of buttons, for instance, have been donated for use in button brooches that the cooperative creates. Less than a year after the idea was voiced, Rosie's guests are not only making the brooches but are also getting into the designing, packaging, and marketing of the product. Twelve women are working three afternoons a week to produce the jewelry, mostly with donated buttons, and the proceeds are going back into the cooperative. The one-of-a-kind pins are being sold at Rosie's Place events, gift shows, Frugal Fannie's Fashion Warehouse, Filene's Basement in downtown Boston, and other retail outlets.

"Being in this environment is being in its abundance," Brandlen says. "We are blessed to have resources to provide well for the women. We give the highest quality we can find in all departments, starting with real juice and organic vegetables in the dining room. We want to give choices, because it may be the only time these women get a choice. They can come here and make some decisions about their lives."

A NOTE FROM THE FOUNDER

ONE WEEK AFTER OUR TENTH anniversary in our first real house, we were, in the lexicon of the 'hood, torched. We saw ten years of our lives swirling around in a fiery mass of curtains, floors, and furniture. The brand-new kitchen was gone. Later that Sunday night, I looked at the almost gutted town house and swore we would be back in a year—bigger, brighter, and better than ever.

The following morning, then Governor Michael Dukakis showed up to commiserate, as about fifty of us were pulling the remaining stuff out of the smoldering mess. Anything that was salvageable, we grabbed. Two days later, I went back into the building and found, stuffed into the remains of the slotted brass mail drop, a piece of brown paper towel. Written on it with a ballpoint pen, painfully relevant, were these lyrics:

> *Each evening from December to December,*
> *Before you drift to sleep upon your cot,*
> *Think back on all the tales that you remember*
> *Of Camelot.*

I wondered. Was this written by a guest or a volunteer? Was it written by someone who really knew us and what we were trying to do? We tacked it up on the walls of the apartment given to us by the Sisters of the Sacred Heart on Shawmut Avenue, an office that was to serve our needs for the next year. The phrase from that song offered quiet inspiration to us as we picked up the pieces of our lives and started all over again.

The following year, to the day, we returned to our town house, but this time we had a plan for a bigger Rosie's Place. We already had one permanent residence; we would turn the town house into a second permanent home for women; and we would move the offices and overnight program to 889 Harrison Avenue. This was the old site of St. Philip's parish, where I had begun my own journey in 1968 as an urban minister.

Not taking a dime from the city, state, or federal government, we have done it our way. We have moved from being a shelter to becoming part of the solution. We are not required to pay property taxes on our houses, but we pay them. This amazes the Boston City Council, but to us, this is being part of the neighborhood. We lobby for new sidewalks, for instance, or for more police protection to get the crack dealers off the street. We pay our share.

Becoming a part of the solution took us a long time to put in place. There is still a frightful need for shelters, but I did not want us to become part of the shelter system, and we fought hard to get out of it. We did it one woman at a time, and no woman will be left out of the loop in our house. Each woman is precious, valuable, important to us. She is our sister, our mother, our child. Thanks to the public who support us, Rosie's Place will continue to strive for the liberation of all women who come through the door. My own personal aspiration is this, a line from Isaiah: "You shall be called the repairer of the breach, the restorer of streets to dwell in."

The day after the fire, in 1984, as we were sorting through the debris, we heard a toot-toot-toot overhead. It was the elevated train that ran by Rosie's Place, the "orange line," since torn down. As we looked up, the driver and the riders gave us thumbs up. We returned the signal, and the train started up again with a clatter, continuing its run.

I remember thinking, "Rosie's Place belongs to all of us. This is their house that went up in flames last night. People will help us."

Moving to 889 Harrison Avenue, we knew we would be taking on a piece of real estate that would cost us more than a million dollars. Could we do it? Within two years, we had the mortgage paid off, and we are still running, still part of the solution, still prisoners of hope.

KIP TIERNAN
JUNE 1997

INDEX